**The Author —
Dr. Margaret Arkinstall,
Physician, Counsellor, and Friend.**

*We remember you in the mission hospital,
  steady, calm, reassuring, skilled,
with warm smile and gentle hands
  ministering . . . physically, emotionally,
spiritually,
  rejoicing with those who held a new life
in their arms
  and weeping with those who faced loss
and grief.*

A beloved physician.

*We remember you in the church,
  leading in worship,
planning musical evenings,
  working with W.M.S. and W.A.,
giving enthusiastic support to the new
  U.C.W.,
encouraging and challenging children and
  youth,
ministering to the minister and his family
  in so many caring ways.*

A joyous, hopeful fellow-pilgrim.

*We remember you in your home,
  a gracious, unhurried hostess
whether the guests numbered two or
  thirty-two,
ready always to welcome a stranger,
  to listen to the troubled or the homesick,
to provide recipes and advice for new
  brides,
holding "open house" for C.G.I.T.
  campers,
for congregational carol-singing,
  for committees of all shapes and sizes.*

A GOOD neighbour.

*And when we remember you
  We join in giving thanks
for having known you,
  for the shared laughter and tears,
for the shared tasks and dreams,
  for the shared memories and hopes.*

*But above all
  for the treasured gift of your friendship.*

Genevieve Carder.

PREFACE

This is the story of a frontier town and its surrounding territory. Many were the pioneers who came to this northland and had a part in its development. Some stayed only a short time, some stayed for years, and some are still there. They came to fulfil many roles - railwaymen, storekeepers, hotel owners, pulp cutters, farmers, trappers, ministers of the gospel, teachers, doctors, nurses, all partners in opening up a new part of Canada. The story is particularly about three of these pioneer partners.

The contents of this book were compiled and written by Dr. Margaret Arkinstall and Elizabeth Pearce from letters written by Dr. William Arkinstall and Margaret (Gretta Mustard) Crookes, an Epic written in 1941 by G. Watt Smith M.A., D.D. (Dr. Margaret's father) and newspaper clippings. The chapter on the Mennonite Settlement was written by John Enns. The cover was designed and drawn by Lee Anne Pearce, grand-daughter of Gretta Crookes.

It is hoped that the readers of this book will gain a greater understanding of the word 'Pioneer'. The Oxford Dictionary defines Pioneer as: 'One who goes before to prepare the way'. Through their lives they have done just that.

ACKNOWLEDGMENTS

* In loving memory of Bill and Gretta *

Acknowledgments to my four children who read the manuscript and made many helpful suggestions; and especially to Elizabeth Pearce who did all the typing, patiently and cheerfully, making as many changes as I requested, arranged for the printing and all the required technicalities. When occasionally it seemed as if we had undertaken too difficult a project, Elizabeth's unfailing enthusiasm, confidence and encouragement kept me at the job. - M.A.

To my husband, Norman, and family for giving me the time to work on this book and to Auntie Margaret, for without her literary skills and memory this book would not have been possible. - E.P.

A sincere thank you to Mrs. Jessie Turner for proof-reading this story for us before its printing - for her kind words of encouragement and best wishes. To Mr. Ron Baker of Impressions Printing who aided these novice publishers with his untiring cooperation and advice on printing layout, thank you. - M.A. and E.P. -

INTRODUCTION

"A long time ago, I dreamed about being up in the north country with the lumberjacks, but not as a doctor. I still love the woods and I can't say just what it is that thrills me when I get out among the trees with the spongy moss under foot, but there is a thrill in a new country, in buzzing down a railway track with a long row of crimson purple fireweed on either side, in seeing the chipmunks and rabbits scurry for cover, in going along in the dark night, with the spruce and poplar and birch forests close on either side, seeing a real moose standing staring with eyes like fire balls, and then seeing another thick chested bull moose gliding across the track one hundred yards in front."

- Dr. William Arkinstall -

* * * *

"There is a great love in our hearts for the north-land part of our country that can never be pushed aside. We appreciate the ease with which we now live compared to the north but no sense of easy living can take away the challenge that was ours."

- Margaret (Gretta Mustard) Crookes -

INDEX

History .... 1.
Teens to College .... 5.
"Stick Your Hat on Your Head" .... 8.
"W.C. Arkinstall M.D., C.M." .... 14.
Pioneers from Afar .... 20.
The Doctor Takes a Wife .... 34.
Gretta .... 40.
Nursing Report to the W.M.S. .... 45.
Modes of Transportation .... 50.
Doug .... 57.
Unforgettable Patients .... 62.
Auntie .... 69.
Camp Athol .... 73.
Parties and Fun .... 88.
Hospital Children .... 97.
British Interlude .... 106.
My Father and Mother .... 108.
"Oscar" .... 113.
Hand in Hand .... 117.
Persuasive Powers .... 126.
A Night at St. Paul's .... 128.
"Inasmuch as ye have done it" .... 131.
Personal Glimpses .... 140.
Rebels With a Cause .... 151.
Two Beginnings .... 154.
Final Additions .... 157.
"In God's Hands" .... 165.
Family Life .... 167.
Ontario Adventure .... 174.
Kapuskasing .... 177.
Arkindale .... 180.
Hôpital Notre Dame .... 184.
The Last Sermon .... 186.

HISTORY

1.

The first settlers came to Hearst in 1911, then
known as Mattawishkwia, named from the river that
flows just east of the town. It was a railway term-
inal and was soon given the name of Grant after a man

who was connected with the railway. Later when the
town was growing and was becoming a place actually on
the map, Sir William Hearst was pleased to give it his
name. Hearst was incorporated as a town in 1922.
The need for some hospital accommodation was first
advocated by a doctor whose name is fast disappearing
into the shades of history, Dr. A.L. Kinsey, who was in
every respect a pioneer, tramping miles carrying his
pack, performing operations under the most primitive
conditions with such help as he could command, trained
or otherwise. The railroad was not completed when
Dr. Kinsey arrived in Hearst. The spirit of adventure
must have been very strong in him, for to reach his
destination, he walked with his packsack from Franz,
the end of the railroad, one hundred miles south of
Hearst. In the 1918 flu epidemic he did a tremendous
job, going about on foot from house to house day and
night, in his bush clothing and high boots, saving
many a life. Tragically, he was unable to save his
wife and three children, all of whom succumbed to the
disease in the short space of twenty-four hours. The
doctor constructed a small building on the lot on Front

Street where his residence stood, a boon to the sick
and suffering in those early days. This was actually
the first hospital in Hearst. Following the loss of
his wife and children, Hearst was never the same for
him and he stayed only a short time afterwards. When
he left he donated not only his surgical instruments
to the hospital but also the more intangible inspiration of his courageous contribution to this frontier
land. Following Dr. Kinsey was Dr. Quackenbush, who
was able to travel all the way in comparative comfort,
on a train. He stayed three to four years and was succeeded by Dr. Molson Cain.

Interest in the northern frontier was growing and
the idea that a more extensive hospital was required
occurred jointly to the Rev. Dr. Byrnes, Superintendent of Home Missions for the Presbyterian Church in
Northern Ontario, and Mrs. H.M. Kipp, who held a
similar position with the Woman's Missionary Society,
more directly as Secretary of Medical Missions in Canada.

A project known as the Forward Movement grew up
from the Presbyterian Church, inspired by the armistice
and the thankfulness for the ending of the First World
War. One feature of the Forward Movement was the
raising of money for different departments of service.
By some means, St. Paul's Church in Ottawa was informed
of the need of a hospital in this new country of
Northern Ontario. A canvass for contributions was
made and $8,000.00 raised for the project. When the
plans and contracts for the building came to be considered this sum proved to be insufficient to meet the
cost of the modest place to be erected, so a further
appeal was made to the congregation to increase their
gifts. By that time, however, there was an agitation on
hand for a union of churches among the Congregational,
Presbyterian and Methodist bodies. St. Paul's congregation was sharply divided on that question and the
request for more money was not entertained. But those
who had sponsored the new venture could not be defeated
and the government of Ontario was approached. The
sponsors pointed out that the cost of the building had
increased due to the rise in wages, making the original
contribution of $8,000.00 insufficient. They appealed
to the government for assistance, and were successful
in their appeal, the government agreeing to contribute
$2,000.00 at once and a further sum of $2,000.00 at a

St. Paul's Hospital (left)
1920 - 1921
St. Paul's Presbyterian Church
(below)

later date.

Eight lots of crown land were given for the construction of the hospital and the property was transferred to the Woman's Missionary Society, who became owners of the hospital. They continued to hold that relation which is shown by the sign over the main entrance, "St. Paul's Hospital Woman's Missionary Society", named after St. Paul's Church in Ottawa.

They considered themselves most venturesome when they made provision for ten beds within their new building. There was sufficient bed space at first, the number of patients seldom exceeding this number; actually on one occasion there was but one patient.

The hospital building was completed in the year 1920-1921 and about the same time the Presbyterian Church was built. It, too, was named St. Paul's. The architect was W.L. Somerville of Toronto, and the builder, Mr. W.E. Powell, one of the most aggressive pioneers of the town. The late Rev. Joseph Irwin M.A., B.D. was the first minister and took as keen an interest in the new hospital as in his new church. In fact much of the success of the building of the hospital was due to his energy. As there was neither orderly nor caretaker, Mr. Irwin made it his job to carry out many mundane duties, such as carrying wood and water into the building. This part of his ministry meant a great deal to the nurses. After his tasks were finished for the day, he would spend some time in the company of the nurses, a friendship which resulted in the marriage of one of them (Miss Willis,) to Mr. Irwin.

The town was growing, more settlers were moving into the area, and people were beginning to make more use of the hospital. It soon became evident that more space was needed, so in 1930 an extension was added, which provided seven additional beds. At the same time a much needed nurses' residence was built which was an integral part of the hospital unit. In contrast to the present time when most nurses have their own homes or apartments, all our nurses at St. Paul's came from out of town and lived in residence. They came to know one another very well which led to intimate relationships, as in a happy family. They did things together in off-duty hours and had a lot of fun.

After Bill graduated from High School, he spent
seven years on the home farm and as he was the eldest
son, he gradually took on more and more responsibility.
It was a dairy farm with registered Holstein cattle
which won many prizes at the exhibitions. When Bill
announced his intention of going to university to study
medicine, it was a bitter disappointment to his father,
who had expected that this would be the son who would
carry on the farm. The day Bill told him, his dad
went off by himself to the barn and wept. There were
two other sons who followed in their father's foot-
steps, one on the home farm, the other on a neigh-
bouring one, as efficiently and ably as their father
before them.

The course of true love does not always run smooth.
Bill and I met when he was eighteen and I was twelve.
My father was the minister at the local church around
which most of our social activities centred. I had
an older sister who was much closer to Bill's age than
I was. The automobile was in its early days and horse
and buggy transportation was still the usual mode.
Girls living in the country were driven by their boy
friends to social events. When Bill invited me to
various functions, my mother insisted that my sister
Mary go too as she considered me too young to go alone
with a boy. Bill soon discovered this and would invite
both of us and Mary, rather reluctantly, would come
along. We had many good times in those years while I
was growing up. My sister died suddenly of heart
failure at age twenty-four a few months before I entered
University. It was a tragic blow to all our family.
Although there were nearly seven years between us the
difference in age had seemed to narrow as we grew older
and we had become great chums.

I had no thought of anything beyond friendship
with Bill but he, six years older, dreamed of a closer
relationship. When he was nineteen or twenty, he was
critically ill with pneumonia. In later years when we
began to exchange intimate confidences he told me that
his main recollection of that illness was knowing that
he might die and thinking, "I don't want to die. I don't

want to leave Margaret." As the years passed, my intuition told me that Bill was in love with me. He was shy and self-conscious when we were together which often irritated me. During our college years we saw one another only during holidays and occasionally at rugby games. When these were in Toronto, Bill would buy a ticket for me along with his own in a block assigned to the Queen's section. This would mean sitting in the 'enemy camp' among all the cheering Queen's students. My voice was like a cry in the wilderness when I cheered for Varsity (my Alma Mater).

As the years passed, our relationship changed very little. As the daughter of the manse, I was well known and invited out by other boys, always going with the one who was the first to ask me. I always felt uncomfortable when I had to tell Bill I had already promised someone else as I could sense his disappointment. Nothing was said about a closer re-lationship between us and by the time we reached our final years at college I decided we could not carry on like that any longer. Trying to analyse my feelings, I thought it was still just friendship with me and romantic love with Bill. I felt I was being unfair to him, leading him on with false hope. After a great deal of mental struggle I wrote a letter to Bill, the most difficult I have ever written, telling him how I felt and suggesting that he seek other girl friends. When the letter had been mailed I thought I would have a sense of relief, but instead, I was miserably un-happy. What had I done? Had I made the biggest mis-take of my life? Bill was deeply hurt and very angry as he later confessed. In a few days his reply came - I was almost afraid to open the envelope. In the letter the hurt was all too evident but not the anger. It was a sad letter thanking me for the happy times we had had through the years and telling me, for the first time, he had dreamed we could spend our lives together. At the end he said, "You have closed the door, and if it is ever to be opened again, you are the one to do it. I have not closed it on my side." Suddenly something happened to me. I had been wretched ever since I wrote the letter, but now my tears were tears of relief. I did love him, I knew it! How could I have been so blindly stupid? I had hurt him terribly, but he had said I could open the door. I

would open it at once! Off went a letter that day -
a very different one this time, humble, remorseful but
happy. At last, I knew my own mind. Bill came to
Toronto as soon as possible. We went for a long walk
and beside the bandstand in Queen's Park, a very pretty
spot, we became engaged. Whenever we were in Toronto
together through the years we always made time to walk
past that place in the park - our betrothal shrine.
    We graduated in 1930, Bill from Queen's and I
from Toronto. Then followed for each of us our interne
year, Bill at the Ottawa Civic and I at the Moose Jaw
General in Saskatchewan. Moose Jaw and Ottawa seemed
a long way apart and we kept the post office busy with
'love' letters. We were both busy and knew that the
months would soon pass.

"STICK YOUR HAT ON YOUR HEAD"

3.

During our college years we had been active in the
Student Volunteer movement and had looked ahead to
serving as missionary doctors in a country overseas.
As time went on and graduation was approaching we
abandoned the idea of going abroad, as it was evident
that my elderly parents would need my help in the not
too distant future. We then began to look at the
various prospects of medical mission work in Canada.
In the last year of college we had thought a good deal
about Bonnyville and Cold Lake, Alberta, where there were
hospitals under the W.M.S. served by one doctor. These
two places especially appealed to Bill as he was
familiar with that part of the country having spent
two summers on Student Mission Fields in northern
Alberta during his medical course. The arrangement
there was that the doctor was under the direct employment of the W.M.S. with salary. Bill was of two minds
whether he liked this arrangement, preferring to be
the missionary doctor but more independent. Suddenly,
in April of 1931, which was nearly the end of his
interne year, a letter came to Frank Kinnaird, a fellow
interne, from his cousin Wes McEachern who lived at
Hearst, inquiring if Frank knew of anyone who would be
interested in taking over the job there. Knowing
Bill's interest in a missionary hospital Frank showed
him the letter and Bill was immediately interested.
The doctor who had been at Hearst for some time was
planning to leave and set up practice elsewhere. In
this letter was a great deal of information about the
town and the various duties which a doctor coming in
would be expected to perform, in addition to being the
missionary doctor working at the hospital. There were
several pulp companies with Hearst as their headquarters,
there was the C.N.R. contract, and there was a good
hospital, a small one at the time, belonging to the
Woman's Missionary Society of the United Church. Bill
had an impulsive nature and if an idea came to him
which he thought had merit, he always acted on it at
once. This was no exception.

How could he get some more information at once?
In the capital city with all its offices this should

not be too difficult. He took the afternoon off and
visited the Government Experimental Farm to get what
further information they could supply. He learned
that Hearst was very much a pioneer location, the in-
dustries being pulpwood and railroading. They told
him that at present there was a lull in the pulp industry and the camps. The most encouraging man he met
was Dr. Stone of the Indian Department, a very out-
spoken and cheerful chap. Bill plied him with questions
regarding the closed camps. "Oh well," he said, "they
will open again. They'll be cutting pulpwood inside
two years. This depression isn't going to last forever."
He told Dr. Stone he was engaged to be married and
queried about the living conditions in Hearst. "Oh,"
he said, "it's a frontier town. Women have lived up
there before. I would say it was all right, but
don't go by me as I don't have a wife." Bill told him
he was thinking of going to Hearst to look the situation
over. He replied, "Good man! Just stick your hat on
your head and go!" With this encouragement, Bill called
Dr. Cain, the company doctor, who was still in Hearst.
He was very eager to sell his practice and advised Bill
to go to Toronto where he would meet the Chief Sanitary
Inspector, Mr. Wilson, and Dr. J.P. Mitchell of the
C.N. Railways. Dr. Cain urged him to leave right away
as there were other people interested in the pulpwood
practice at Hearst. From the Experimental Farm Bill
phoned the Civic Hospital secretary, a good pal of his,
and asked her to make arrangements for him to leave for
Toronto on the night train. He ran to catch the street-
car, borrowed two shirts, some BVDs, socks and money
from his buddy, Stan Trenouth, another interne. The
hospital night operator called a taxi and at midnight
he was en route to Toronto on the first lap to the North
Country, fifteen hours after Frank had shown him his
cousin's letter.

In Toronto he received the same attention from Mr.
Wilson as Dr. Stone had given him. As soon as he affirmed
his intention of going to Hearst interest was aroused.
He said, "You are the first man I have talked to who
said he would go to Hearst. I think I can tell you now
that if you go there we will recommend your appointment
as doctor for the camps in that area, including a ten
dollar monthly fee per camp for sanitary inspection
supervision." Dr. J.P. Wilson also was most cordial

and invited Bill to his office for consultation. Things were moving fast; before noon he was medical represent- ative for the three pulp camps which employed thirty men in one camp to two hundred in another, and Medical Officer for the C.N. Railway, which included a full time pass from Hearst to Toronto and from Hearst to Nakina. A little later he received a contract with the Algoma Central Railway and was appointed examiner for nearly all the insurance companies who had any work in the town.

He was running very short of funds and after a snack at the railway station, called on Janet Little, a good Queen's University friend, spent the evening and stayed long enough so that she was obliged to feed him. He slept in the station waiting room overnight, leaving on the morning train for Sault Ste. Marie. His sister Kate, a teacher there, met him at the station and said, "Bill, let's go and have something to eat." He said, "That's fine. I am ready for lunch and you'll have to pay for it, too, as I am broke." His sister was slight- ly upset by this bold statement but obliged and he had a good meal at her expense.

Bill arrived in Hearst April 21st, 1931 by the night train which always got in just after eleven. That night he spent at the Waverly Hotel across from the station and the next morning arranged with Mrs. Sharp, the proprietress, for room and board for the summer. There was a foot of snow which had just fallen the previous day. As Bill describes it in his first letter to his parents - "Up at seven o'clock for a walk before Dr. Cain got up. It looks like a prairie town, everything flat, in the middle of the clay belt, heavy clay sub-soil with moss on top. It takes a few years to get mellow and then it is splendid farming land. About five to ten miles from the town on every side, spruce forest, probably one hundred cars of pulpwood piled up around the freight yard. The town is scattered; there are a number of nice bungalow houses, a nice United Church Hospital, seventeen beds, four graduate nurses, a French doctor who is a good man and has been here for several years. He has a large practice, mainly French people.

Dr. Aubin

Map of Hearst copied from
Bill's first letter to his parents -

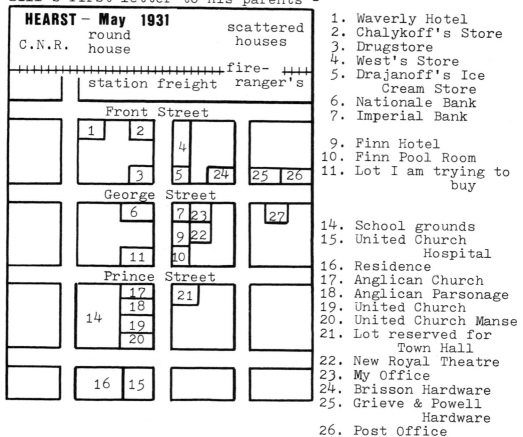

HEARST – May 1931

C.N.R. round house — scattered houses

station freight — fire-ranger's

Front Street

1 2

4

3 5 24 25 26

George Street

6 7 23

9 22

11 10 27

Prince Street

17 21

18

14 19

20

16 15

1. Waverly Hotel
2. Chalykoff's Store
3. Drugstore
4. West's Store
5. Drajanoff's Ice
   Cream Store
6. Nationale Bank
7. Imperial Bank

9. Finn Hotel
10. Finn Pool Room
11. Lot I am trying to
    buy

14. School grounds
15. United Church
    Hospital
16. Residence
17. Anglican Church
18. Anglican Parsonage
19. United Church
20. United Church Manse
21. Lot reserved for
    Town Hall
22. New Royal Theatre
23. My Office
24. Brisson Hardware
25. Grieve & Powell
    Hardware
26. Post Office
27. Powell House

George Street, 1931

There is a United Church nearby, there is a movie theatre, there are sixteen places to sleep and eat showing how transient the population is. There is not one vacant house and eight new ones are going up in Hearst this summer. There are public and separate schools and a convent. There are six to ten stores in town, two with a stock of $40,000.00, one handling about twenty-five cars of potatoes in a year. A new Experimental Farm has been started on the edge of town and there will be $20,000.00 to $30,000.00 spent there this summer and probably the same next year. Hearst will probably be a quiet town but still a good one. The population now is perhaps eight hundred."

Bill met Dr. Cain, who showed him his office, a very tidy one at the front of the theatre. That night a double party was given, a farewell for Dr. Cain and a welcome for the new doctor. He purchased Dr. Cain's practice and engaged his "beautiful Swedish secretary" who piloted Bill through the first months of practice at Hearst.

Dr. Cain had worked up an excellent practice, having been in the town for ten years. Mrs. Cain did not share the pioneer spirit of her husband. When she arrived in Hearst she hated this frontier town and refused to stay so that the doctor had been living as a bachelor all this time. He had made enough money to buy a house in Toronto where his wife and two girls were living. Now he had been offered the position of resident houseman in Toronto Western Hospital with a position on the university staff. He had achieved his goal, that of making enough money to feel secure and was anxious to join his wife and family and set up a real home.

Now that Bill had made his commitment to practise in Hearst, the information he had procured before his arrival, together with what he had learned from Dr. Cain and his impression of the town and hospital, reassured him that this was the place where he wanted to settle rather than Alberta. Quoting from a letter to his parents - "This is the first opening that I have had to earn sure money and to do work that I like. I am going to be in a position to help those that have done so much for me. There is much more missionary work to be done here than in Bonnyville and Cold Lake and I can do better social and church work here as an independent, self-supporting doctor than I could at Bonnyville on salary. Here I will be doing it because I want to do it, not because it is expected of me. I am going to get married, I want to have a home, keep out of debt and be independent. I have met the mayor, a fine man and a number of other very fine and very friendly people, so I think we can be happy here even if it is a shabby, muddy, scattered, snowbound frontier town in northern Ontario. As things go now, my expenses will be - office $40.00 - office girl $60.00 - room $25.00 - board $25.00 - post office box $2.00 - insurance $7.00 - laundry $5.00 - Total $164.00 a month. This first month I won't make any more than that but the second month I should more than double or triple my income. The previous doctor is a very fine man but has run his practice on a straight business basis - no pay, no service. We can't do that, but we will be sure of a very good living and plenty to pay our debts with so much camp work. (My secretary continually chides me for not charging the patients enough)."

In these days of increasing medicare payments, compare our income in the 1930's. The total business for June was $482.87 plus Compensation fees amounting to about $50.00. Income for July $540.00. The practice for the month of August was estimated to be about $900.00.

I spent all that summer of 1931 completing my
internship in Moose Jaw and my first introduction to
Hearst was through Bill's letters.

"As the pulp camps are closed there is less
surgery than I expected, as naturally there are no
pulp cutters' accidents in the woods. The maternity
business is very active, also the children's ward;
there are few elderly folk in this new country."

His first patient was an old man who was living
in his hen house after his house had burned down. He
became ill from eating the crust of porridge from his
partially dried porridge pot. He recovered quickly
after one day's stay in hospital.

Another early patient was a little girl with
strychnine poisoning from eating rat poison. Bill was
called to her home to see her and found her on the
verge of convulsions. There was no time to move her
to the hospital. He sent to the hospital for ether
and other medications, then realized that inflammable
ether could not be used in lamp light, so he sent for
chloroform. In the meantime he was treating the little
girl trying to get her to vomit. At last when the
proper medication arrived he was able very quickly
to anaesthetize with chloroform, pass the stomach tube
and get her to bring up everything. Her recovery was
almost instantaneous, since strychnine leaves no
after-effects once the poison is gone. This had happened late at night. The next morning Bill went to
see her and found her running around after having had
a good breakfast contrary to orders, which were that
she was to have only clear fluids until he saw her.

Two other patients that summer were seven month
premature babies, both of whom Bill delivered in their
homes. One belonged to a Finnish family where they had
only boys and were anxious for a little girl and this
little baby was a girl. She was so tiny; in his letter
describing her to me he said, "Her head was the size
of an orange and a small one at that." As she was
delivered at home he had no accurate scales with which
to weigh her but judged that she was under two pounds.
It was summer time and really warm weather. The mother

stayed in bed with the baby so as to act as an incubator, keeping the baby warm, feeding her breast milk with a medicine dropper. Her husband was a wonderful house-keeper and nurse, took care of the mother and baby for the length of time necessary to incubate the baby. That little girl did very well. Years afterwards when we went back to Hearst, we saw her, a lovely young woman.

An amusing incident Bill wrote to me about that summer concerned a maternity patient in the country to be confined at home. While he was waiting for the baby to be delivered, the woman's husband told him that he had a sick cow. Bill went out to the barn with the man to see the cow which had a bruised fore-tit. He advised the owner what to do, told him how to do it then came back into the house to wait until it was time to deliver the baby. Everything went well with both the mother and the baby. A few days later when Bill went back to see his patients, the man asked him how much it would be. He had intended charging $35.00 for cases in the country but seeing the poverty in that home he made his charge $25.00. The man was delighted. He said, "You're a good doctor. Missus is all right, the baby's all right, cow's all right."

Not all his early cases turned out happily; indeed one had a tragic ending. He got a call about midnight to go to Savoff - sixty miles west of Hearst. Three people had been seriously injured when the motor car 'speeder', the only means of transportation, struck a moose on the railway track. There was no highway. Bill arrived about two a.m. on a 'speeder' to find a young man, twenty-one years of age, unconscious with definite signs of compression. The woman's face was badly bruised, a ragged cut on her forehead and a cut on her lip. Her husband had a lacerated nose. There was nothing for it but to treat the patients right there beside the railroad track. The train was due at four a.m. which meant that there were two hours to wait during which time he gave the woman an anesthetic by the side of the track while he sutured her lacerations, sutured the wounds in the young man's head and those of the older man. They flagged the train at four a.m. and took all the patients to Kapuskasing as there were no X-ray facilities in Hearst. Nothing could be done for the young man and he died the following night.

It was a traumatic experience for a young doctor, the first patient he had lost in his four months of practice.

Hearst is situated in the great clay belt, a crescent shaped basin of deep clay soil located south of James Bay in northwest Ontario and northeast Quebec. It consists of 16,600,00 acres of clay soil with stretches of light sandy soil and boggy areas which become rich muck when cleared and drained. Natural drainage is poor in many areas but with improvements in tile drainage the land could be made much more productive. The growing season is short, ninety or less frost free days. The winters are long with lots of snow, but the long summer days and abundant moisture provide ideal growing conditions for most short season crops. In addition to

hay and grain the soil is ideal for vegetables. Root crops like cabbage, cauliflower, brussels sprouts and broccoli are well adapted to the north, also small fruits like strawberries and raspberries. We found that the climate was not suitable for everything. One year Bill tried crabapples because they are hardy. After two or three years he had two healthy trees bearing blossoms in the spring and we looked forward to a crop of apples if only the frost did not kill the blossoms. Sure enough in due time there were twenty or so apples on the trees. We watched them grow and mature and showed them proudly to all of our visitors. One day when we looked at the trees, to our dismay, the apples were gone - not one left. While looking further we found apples on the ground, some at quite a distance from the trees. What could have happened? There had been no strong wind or storm since yesterday. Then the truth was revealed. I do not know whether Billy confessed or whether an eye witness told but the temptation of those little apples had been too strong for Billy and his friends. They had pulled every one off the branches and thrown them at one another. What did it matter? Twenty apples would have made very little jelly anyway.

In this northern part of the clay belt there are few farms as we know them in southern Ontario. One of these belonged to a man called Johnson, one of the earliest pioneers, who brought in special equipment and cleared about three hundred acres. There was a large family who all worked together, the eldest son, Tom of Little Longlac gold fame*. The mother was one of Bill's early patients, a charming, silver haired pioneer mother. The first time he visited her he walked the mile down the railway track to the homestead.

Bill was enthusiastic about the possibilities of this rich clay belt and prophesied that within twenty-five years the country would be opened up and would be a thriving dairy industry. Unfortunately his prophecy has not been fulfilled as yet. On the other hand, much of the land has grown back into bush, mainly due to the short growing season and the distance from a market. It would now seem likely that eventually, as more and more good farming land in southern Ontario is being replaced by concrete for housing development and industry, the prophecy will come true.

Bill's first impression of Hearst as a quiet town was changed in a short time after he commenced his practice.

The train came in at night, a through train - trans-continental, going out to the west coast. It brought lumberjacks, bootleggers, anyone coming to do business the next day. They would spend that night. The next day they would do their shopping, banking etc., spend another night, and go out on the morning train which left just after six.

In a frontier town like Hearst the police were ever on the alert. When men came to town with their substantial pay cheques with nowhere to spend their idle time except in the beer parlors, fights frequently occurred. A lumberjack was arrested one night and

* Discovered August 1931

17.

thrown into the cell to sober up, which made him very angry, and he resolved to get even with that 'cop' if it took him all summer. It was not long until the opportunity presented itself. He was on a trip down the river several miles from town when the idea struck him. He came straight to town and sought out his enemy (the policeman) and reported that when he was up the river he had seen, "Something in a bag about two feet long - looked like a head at one end - might be an animal, looked like a baby - yes, looked a lot like baby." With such a suspicious account it necessitated an investigation, so the policeman in the company of the magistrate went up the river after getting explicit instructions from the man as to the location of the mysterious parcel. It was blackfly season and the two men were vigorously attacked. Anyone who has been bitten by blackflies will understand. After quite a search they finally found the bag which in fact did look like a baby but when opened up contained a large groundhog. It was hard to say which was worse, their chagrin at being tricked or their swollen blackfly bites. The lumberjack had indeed got his revenge.

There were several bootlegger establishments in town. In addition to supplying liquor to the lumberjacks when they came in, these establishments took advantage of the men. When they were drunk enough to be beyond realizing what was happening they were often robbed by the custodians. Their trips to town would practically always be just after they had received their pay from the pulp camps so they would be carrying a considerable amount of money. There was a Finnish woman in town who owned a 'respectable' bootlegger's business. Certainly she supplied the men with the liquor they requested but demanded their wallets before they went to bed. When they awoke in the morning they were handed their wallets containing all the money except the expenses they had incurred. The men soon learned that this was a safe place to stay.

One of Bill's earliest patients was brought to him with an ugly stab wound from a knife, apparently a commonly used weapon. It was plain to be seen that this was going to be a very different kind of practice from that in a southern Ontario town.

These are his own words in a letter - "This is a tough town; there are things happening here that are

tragic, especially at their dances. There is a liquor
store that does a scandalous business. We will have to
go slowly but I think we should be able to help things
a bit. Perhaps the biggest opportunity is to gather a
group of the best young people together and get them
interested in clean fun and things that are worthwhile."
Bill had always loved horses and was a skillful
rider and driver. He found plenty of opportunity for
riding at Hearst, which was a 'sporty' town with a good
race track. He acquired a standard bred running horse
called 'Beauty' which he trained for the races on July
1st. In his words, "Sorry to be so long in writing.
You will be thinking that I may be hurt in my broncho
busting. Well, I wasn't. I rode in the races. The
first time the saddle shifted and I rolled off as it
slipped underneath. Next heat I rode bare back and
almost fell off but finished a close second. Third
heat, I rode bare back and finished first, so that I
won second over all for the day. I had a lot of
friends that day because a number of people had bet
on my horse. They were mad that I hadn't won first.
Well it didn't spoil my business because I have been
very busy since July 1st." July 1st celebrations in
Hearst were known as Gala Days, with parades, horse
races and other community fun activities. Bill
also indulged in sulky racing at any opportunity. On
one occasion he entered in a sulky race in which there
were four participants. He was the winner!

Bill displays his skill at
sulky racing

Exhibiting the natural
beauty of his animal

There were many nationalities in town. In addition to Anglo Saxons and French, of which the latter
were in the majority, were Finnish, Czechoslovakians,
Mennonites, Swedish, Ukrainian, Polish and a few
Indians.

There emigrated to this rugged north country two
groups of pioneers with whom we were intimately
associated, both as patients and friends. Sixty
Czechoslovakian families came from their country in
the early 1920's and settled about ten miles from
Hearst. They went right into the depth of the woods
hoping to make their homes there. Each man had from
fifty to seventy-five acres of bush land. He was
given by the Government the right to cut a certain
amount of bush for pulpwood for sale each year. They
cleared a little plot of bush, big enough for a little
log cabin to keep them sheltered until they could build
more. The more energetic ones squared their logs, and
made their own shingles, about all they bought being
the glass for the windows. 'They made their own furniture
-tables, chairs, beds and other household articles.

Czechoslovakian
Farm

The other group were Mennonites. Their story
follows, an excerpt from a history of the Mennonite
settlement at Reesor written by John Enns. Reesor
is situated thirty miles from Hearst.

The Story of the Mennonite Settlement of Reesor, Ontario -
Motives for Homesteading and Early Investigations
The settlement of a number of homesteads in Northern
Ontario by a group of Mennonite settlers in the first
quarter of the twentieth century was, for the times, a
somewhat unique and anachronistic development. It had
its remote causes in the Russian revolution of 1917.
This political upheaval robbed these people of their
earthly possessions and so thoroughly convinced them of
the intolerable situation under Communist dictatorship
that they spared no efforts to obtain permission to leave
the country. Emigration became possible in 1923 when
this permission was granted, and when Canadian Mennonites
succeeded in persuading the Canadian Pacific Railways to
transport the thousands of immigrants on a unique and
generous credit arrangement. Between 1923 and 1930,
some 20,000 Mennonites left Russia and emigrated to
Canada. Almost without exception, the settlers of
Reesor came from this large group, who had found their
first temporary homes in the provinces of Ontario,
Manitoba, Saskatchewan and Alberta.
On the steppes of Russia these immigrants had lived
in villages or, in some cases, on individual farms. Only
a few families had become urbanized in the last gener-
ation and had lived in towns. However, all of them were
still in very close touch with the traditions of
European rural community life and the occupation of
most of them had been farming on their own land, special-
izing in the production of wheat.
Those who came to the western provinces found themselves in circumstances much like those they had left,
except for the absence of the traditional village organization, and for the necessity of adapting to new ethnic
surroundings. On the western wheat farms there was
little opportunity for employment outside of the harvest
season, and the newcomers were practically forced by
circumstances to buy farms on share payments or on credit
to survive at all. They were thus able to take up the
same occupation they had had in their old home, but they
shouldered tremendous debts which, at that time, seemed
almost insurmountable. While, in one way, they were
happy once more on their "own" piece of land, growing
wheat, they were deeply alarmed at the prospect of for-

ever remaining paupers, succeeding merely in meeting the
interest on their huge land debts.

The group that came to Ontario found themselves in
quite unwonted surroundings. Here they were dispersed
among the rural homes of their co-religionists, many of
whom even spoke their own German language, but as these
farmers lived on individual farms, the economy had a
different base, being mixed farming and serving the many
industrial towns of Ontario's south. There were year-
long employment possibilities on these farms but wages
were low and the continued dependence of the entire
family on the employing farmers was not to the liking
of these individualistic people. The average Ontario
farmer could not afford to employ more than one farm-
hand on a yearly basis and most of the immigrant families
were split up, members above school age working on different farms, able to meet only on Sundays. Although
grateful for the reception they received and for the
shelter and income these farm jobs offered during the
early period of their stay in Canada, most families
began drifting into towns after a year or two, when
factory jobs offered better pay, where they could enjoy
a measure of independence, and above all, where families
could stay together. For some families this was the
final solution to the problem of finding a permanent
home and of adjusting to conditions in their new home-
land. But to others, working by the hour and punching
time-clocks in a factory was obnoxious in the extreme.
They feared the influence of the factory milieu on their
children, thinking that, in the long run, it would
inevitably lead to their proletarianization. They
tolerated all this for a while because, after all, there
was a debt to pay to the C.P.R. and a nest egg to be
provided for a new home, but all their lives they had
been masters in their own little domains, and this goal
of again establishing their own independent holdings,
where they and their children could be masters of their
own time, was never allowed to get out of sight. They
heard of their friends buying wheat farms out west, but
they were afraid of the possible consequences of contract-
ing unmanageable debts. More and more, with some of them,
the idea gained ground that the best way to make a new
beginning would be to settle on virgin soil, on land
that was cheap and would offer possibilities for the

establishment of closed communities, after the pattern of their colonies in Russia.

It was at this stage that their attention was drawn to the possibility of homesteading in Northern Ontario. A man by the name of Jacob Siemens of Winnipeg, probably a land agent, offered free tickets to a delegation, should they want to go north to have a look at the homesteads that were available in the District of Cochrane.

During the month of January, 1925, two men, accompanied by Siemens, went north and looked over the proposed area. They could not make a proper appraisal of the land because of the heavy cover of snow upon it, but they noted the thick stands of spruce pulpwood on the land and could well estimate that in this the prospective settlers would have a reliable source of income for a considerable period of time, during which they would be able to clear land for future farming.

When the delegates returned and reported their findings to a meeting, the majority of those present decided against settling in the northern forest. Dreading the prospect of having to pull stumps, a task neither their forefathers nor they had ever tackled, they judged it to be more advantageous to make a new beginning on the western prairie lands.

However, a man by the name of Thomas Reesor, a minister and leader in an old Mennonite congregation in the vicinity of Pickering, Ontario, whose forebears had cleared land in southern Ontario, had great faith in the possibilities that wooded homesteads offered and he suggested that those who did not want to go west, should give it a try. He offered to obtain free settlers' tickets from the C.N.R. for another inspection tour in the spring. This offer was accepted by a group of interested people and at the beginning of May of the same year four men went north for another look. Walking through the beautiful spring forest, with trees just breaking into leaf, and the swarms of mosquitoes and blackflies as yet unhatched, the four men came to the tentative decision to give it a try, provided they could obtain a goodly number of other interested people to join them. The settlement was named after Thomas Reesor.

When they returned from this trip, a call for volunteers was published in the German Mennonite weekly "Die Rundschau", whereupon a considerable number of applications were received to join in the venture.

All these interested people were summoned to a
meeting in Waterloo for the purpose of consolidating
plans to get the settlement underway. About thirty
prospective settlers showed up and the meeting decided
that all those who wanted to settle in the proposed area
were to be in Toronto on the 15th of June, 1925, whence
they would jointly depart to the allotted homesteads in
the north.

A Beginning is Made

On the appointed day a group assembled at the
Toronto station, but only nine heads of families had
shown up, some alone, others with their entire families
or with only a few of their children, those old enough
to help. Mr. Thomas Reesor joined the group as guide
and advisor and the venture of the actual settlement was
under way. As settlers, the group had free passage on
the train.

Although most homesteads in the Cochrane district
that lay within a short distance of the railway lines had
been taken up by this time, there was a stretch between
the stations of Lowther and Macbey (later Parthia), a
distance of seven miles, in which no settlers had hither-
to taken up land. Here the government opened up an
assigned area for settlement by the Mennonites, promising
not to allow anyone else to take up land for a number of
years, until the initial group had had a chance to
assemble as many settlers of their own kind as they could,
to constitute a viable community.

In 1925 the railway was the only means of transportation traversing this complex of land. The gravel road
that led west from Kapuskasing went only as far as the
village of Opasatika and the one that led east from
Hearst did not proceed beyond Mattice, leaving a gap of
nineteen miles. The area to be settled was situated
seven miles east of Mattice and twelve miles west of
Opasatika. At that time two passenger trains served the
area, the 'local' which travelled between Hearst and
Cochrane and the 'express', a through train, connecting
Winnipeg and Quebec City. The local was a flag train
that could be flagged to a stop at any settlement or
flag station. It passed the place of settlement at
seven a.m. going east to Kapuskasing, and again at
approximately eight p.m., returning to Hearst. The

express stopped only at stations manned by an agent. It came by at eleven p.m. going east and again at eleven p.m. going west. It could be made to stop anywhere on special permission from the division superintendent at Cochrane, in order to let off settlers, or for other urgent reasons.

Miss Erna Töws, then only fourteen years old, now Mrs. Peter Dyck of Leamington, Ontario, has written a short retrospect of those first weeks in the bush, which follows below:

"I was fourteen and my brother Cornelius was fifteen years old, when my father took the two of us to the north where, together with a group of Mennonite men, we were to help establish a new settlement. I do not recall the exact point of our departure, but this much I remember, we travelled by train. About midnight, on the second night underway, the train stopped in the wilderness and our group of men got off. As a temporary arrangement, I was put in the care of the Warkentin family, which went on to the next station, in the village of Mattice. Here we were met by a certain Mr. Christianson who, lantern in hand, guided us over a long railway bridge towards the other side of the wide river. It was a very dark and high airy bridge, floored by widely spaced ties and unprotected by side-rails. Its crossing was frightening and seemed interminable. When we finally got to the other side, we found shelter in a small cabin, owned by Mr. Christianson, where I remained for a week with Mrs. Warkentin and her children.

In the meantime, our group of men, left by the train at the edge of an endless forest, stood around for a while in the dark, forlorn and crestfallen. For shelter, they had brought only one small tent. This was soon put up, but alas, it could only admit a few of them. The others had to make do with what scant protection was offered by the trees. They became the helpless prey of mosquitoes and blackflies, for it was the month of June, when these pests are at their worst. Only with the dawning of the new day did they discover a vacant log cabin quite nearby.

This cabin had solid log walls and a roof and there were openings in the walls for windows and an entrance but these contained no sash and glass and no door. The newcomers did not know who owned the cabin, but, seeing that it was abandoned, they appropriated it for a temp-

orary home. In a week's time my father came for me and
brought me to his makeshift abode. Thus I became the
first female of this settlement. All of us slept on
the ground, for the cabin had no wooden floor. Moss
was fetched from the forest to serve for mattresses
and logs were laid on the moss layer to mark off the
individual sleeping areas, so that each one could know
the extent to which he could stretch and roll. I was
assigned a 'stall' in the farthest corner of the cabin,
where I could hide behind my father and brother. How
glad I was in those days to have the security and assur-
ance of their protective presence!

One by one the men selected homesteads for themselves and got them registered in their names. When
this was done, they began building on their own lands,
usually working in pairs, since one man could not
handle the heavy logs alone. In the evenings, however,
they all came back to the shelter of the cabin and we
would sit beside the fire which was built on the bare
ground in the middle of the cabin. Naturally, the room
was always filled with smoke, for we had no chimney and,
besides, we needed the smoke to keep the mosquitoes from
eating us alive. In this way we ate our suppers in the
evenings and listened to the stories these men had to
tell. They had come from various parts of Russia and
had come through a lot of harrowing experiences during
the troubled years of the Russian revolution. Some
tales were sad enough to move me to tears, while others
were exceedingly funny. When we sat beside our makeshift tables and partook of the meals we had cooked over
the open fire, rabbits and sqirrels would come right
into our midst to snatch food remnants that were thrown
to them. They had no fear, for they had not yet come to
know man. Partridges would at times sit close to the
door and would not move, until they were dropped by a
thrown stone or stick, to be added to the food supply.
Nature was as free and unspoiled as God had made it.

During the daytime the men were usually away,
working on their own homesteads. Then I was alone in
the cabin. One day one of the men, Mr. Jacob Heinrichs
came back early, palefaced and reeling. What had
happened? He had cut a deep gash into his leg with the
axe. I stood there helpless, not knowing what to do.
We did not have a thing for dressing wounds. Nothing!
Then I saw him take a bottle of liniment and pour some of

it into the open cut. Seeing the poor man bend double
with pain, I thought his end had come! He remained in
the cabin for a few days and then went back to work
again. Thus the days passed.

My father had chosen his homestead quite close to
the cabin and soon discovered that someone, probably a
trapper, in days gone by, had left a little log shanty
on it. It had a flat slanting roof, only one window and
a door, but it was something that belonged to us and my
father, brother and I lost no time in moving into it.
We were quite elated over the fact that we would now be
able to live in our own cabin in privacy. Here I could
run my own little household. I cooked, baked and did
our laundry and in spare hours, walked over to the building site, some two hundred yards away, to help with the
construction of the house. I do not know where Dad got
hold of the two-wheeled chassis he had at the site,
which we used to transport the newly-cut spruce logs
to the building site. We would put the heavy end of the
log on the axle bar. Dad would hold up the smaller end,
and thus, with Cornelius and me pulling at the tongue
or shaft, we would transport each log to where we wanted
it at the site. It took many logs to build the two
storey house we needed for our family of ten. The logs
were carefully fitted one upon another, the chinks between them were filled with moss and then sealed and
smoothed with a slurry of clay. Houses thus constructed
were warm. Later when strips of strong building paper
were tacked over the inner side of the wall and this in
turn was covered with printed wall-paper, the rooms
became quite presentable. At first, however, everything
was very primitive.

One day, after the main house walls stood ten feet
high and we were busy on the gable and roof section, Dad
slipped on a beam and fell, hitting the upper rim of the
wall with his chest. He became very sick almost at once.
A bad night followed. I could not sleep, for Dad seemed
seriously ill. It was impossible to call a doctor, for
the nearest one was thirty miles away and there were no
roads. I sat at my father's bedside, desperate and very
quiet. Suddenly he spoke and said, "Should I die here,
take my fondest greetings to Mother, will you? I was
very sad, feeling helpless and hopeless. But a miracle
happened! Dad spent a few days on his sickbed in the
shanty, then got up and continued to work on the house.

Later it was discovered that he had fractured two ribs.

Otherwise the days went by uneventfully. All parties worked diligently at their houses, to have them ready for the first cold weather in the fall. Our provisions had to be packed in from Mattice, seven miles away. We walked in on the railway bed, trying to adjust our steps to the varying distances between the ties. Coming back, we carried packsacks containing our purchases. Oh, how tired we used to get on these fourteen mile shopping trips!

When the houses were finally finished after three months of arduous labour, preparations were made to have the families come up from southern Ontario. The wives of the men were notified when and how to leave. A time of anxious waiting set in and the question was often asked: Would the express stop at the new settlement, since there was no station? Dad estimated the day on which the group should arrive. When that day came and train-time approached, we lit a lantern and made off to the railway, determined to flag the train to a stop. Everything seemed to go as expected. The headlight of the train appeared in the distance at the usual time, the lantern was kept in motion, swinging back and forth over the track, and two short whistle blasts indicated that the engineer intended to stop. Our excitement reached a climax when the train ground to a halt, but then, what disappointment! --- none of those we had expected had arrived. We could do nothing else but hope for better luck the next day. I tidied up the house for a second time, for I wanted everything to be in tip-top shape when mother arrived. I baked a batch of raspberry squares from berries that grew wild around the place and, at train time, we were all back at the track again, signalling assiduously with our lantern as on the night before. But this time the train showed no inclination to stop. Whistling loudly and long, as if in derision, it passed us at full speed. We looked at one another in dismay and wondered what could have happened to make plans go awry. "All good things are *trine!" was the best we could say for consolation and the next evening we were all there again. No disappointment that time! The train stopped and all our loved ones came off, one after another. What a joyous reunion it was!

* Word from an old German saying that means on the third. All good things happen on the third time.

From here on things began to go better. Winter soon came and the men began to cut pulpwood for the mill in Kapuskasing, which provided us with much needed income. More young people had arrived and a good deal of visiting and socializing set in, all of which, viewed in retrospect, adds up to many pleasant memories."

After the pioneer group had made themselves reasonably comfortable in their temporary shelters and selected their homesteads, each man gave priority to the task of building a log house on his own half lot of seventy-five acres. For the one-time grain growers from the steppes of Russia this task of constructing log-houses was no simple matter. Their only tools were hammers, axes and Swedish bucksaws, with perhaps a level and a plane thrown in here and there. The Swedish saws, though very efficient in the hands of experts, required great skill for the setting and sharpening of the teeth on the blades and could easily become instruments of heart-breaking frustration and torture in the hands of the uninitiated. Most of the men had probably never felled a tree in their lives. Fortunately, one or two of the men had served their stint in the forests of northern Russia in lieu of military service and were able to demonstrate to the others what were the proper ways of felling trees and how to notch and join logs into house walls. None of the houses had storm windows and during periods of heavy winter frosts the window panes became covered with thick layers of multiflowered hoar-frost. Not one of the houses had a fire-proof chimney. What passed for chimneys for a while were stove pipes extended through the roof, the cause of many a house fire in the years to come.

When autumn arrived, the men had their dwellings finished and were able to have their families come north to join them. They did not all come at the same time, some arriving in September, others as late as November. It should be noted that not all the wives who came north to join their husbands did so with any show of enthusiasm. They had had a taste of the comfortable life possible in the well-developed south and were confident that their families could achieve a very satisfactory standard of living under the prevailing conditions in a very short time. However, to their credit it must be said that, once settled in the primitive surroundings of a pioneer settlement, they made the best of the situation and put up with the initial inconveniences without complaint. The younger members of the families took the change to backwoods living more lightly, more in a spirit of adventure.

The arrival of families of the original group of men, and the coming of additional families from the western provinces and southern Ontario even in the first year made normal family life possible and ushered in the beginnings of community life. The founding fathers had envisaged this, of course, and had not forgotten to make preparations for the latter even while they worked so hard at their building to ensure the earliest possible resumption of the former. One of their first concerns was the establishment of a school section under existing provincial regulations, to ensure that their children would suffer no loss of instruction because of their settling in a remote area. They made the necessary contracts and arrangements for the creation of a new school section, and made determined efforts to obtain a teacher who would be able and willing to give instruction in German and to offer religious instruction in this language in addition to the English programme of studies prescribed by the Department of Education.

They were able to hire a young man, David Heidebrecht, who had recently arrived in Canada and had just completed his Normal School course. When the term opened in September, 1926, the school building was far from complete and Mr. Heidebrecht set up seats and desks in his own living quarters so that there would be no time lost. By Christmas the new schoolhouse was finished and they were able to hold their Christmas concert in it. In addition to teaching day school, Mr. Heidebrecht performed many other services - conducted night school classes, arranged for a post office to be opened, wrote Eatons' orders for people, and helped with clerical tasks. In short, he was the English tongue and English pen of the settlement."

* * * *

After the first few years it became increasingly obvious to these hard working people that their expectations of establishing farms in this new fertile land were doomed to failure as the seventy-five acres allotted to them by the government was totally inadequate. When

the pulpwood was all cut, meaning the end of ready
money, it soon became evident that they could not make
a living on such a small acreage. They were ambitious,
industrious, good farmers, and would have done their
share to open up the country to agriculture. However
as the years passed and the children grew older, these
people realized they must make a change, and made
preparations to leave. A few moved to western Canada,
the majority to southern Ontario, where they have done
exceedingly well. The families in southern Ontario get
together each year for a reunion picnic. As 1975 was
the fiftieth anniversary since the first settlers had
come to Reesor they decided to go back to the original
spot for the reunion that year. Bill and I were present
at the reunion, a very great occasion.

John Enns, to whom I extend my gratitude for allowing me to incorporate into this book his story of the
beginning of the Mennonite settlement at Reesor, is a
retired teacher who taught at the local school some
time following David Heidebrecht. He is the only
Mennonite still living there, and opened up his home and
his fields to the campers when they came to the reunion.
He put up two very handsome outhouses for the occasion,
constructed from the original wood that had been used
for the homestead which his father built in the early
years. The people began to arrive on Friday and stayed
through until Sunday evening or Monday morning, camping
in the field and getting their own meals, using John's
house for anything that they were not able to prepare
with their own camping outfits.

There was a church service outdoors on the Sunday
morning, the minister preaching in German. He was able
to speak English but said he did not feel at home
preaching in English, preferring his native language.
At one point during the sermon, everybody laughed up-
roariously. Bill and I, of course, had no idea what
the joke was and asked afterwards what had been so
funny. This is what the minister had been saying that
caused the great mirth: he was describing the first two
or three families who arrived in Reesor in 1925. They
were put off the train at eleven o'clock at night, in
June, beside the track with no one to meet them. This
was described earlier in Mrs. Peter Dyck's account.
Although no human being was there, there was an enthusiastic welcoming crowd - of mosquitoes. This was what

31.

1975 - Fiftieth
Anniversary of
Reesor settlement
in the fields of
John Enns.

Outdoor Church
service.

had caused the congregation to laugh so heartily. Fifty years later it was funny, but in 1925, as **Mrs.** Dyck writes, it was a forlorn experience.

There is a little cemetery at Reesor, John Enns, its caretaker. It was very neat with the grass freshly cut and flowers planted at the graves. After the regular church service a memorial service was held in the cemetery. There were three generations of people at the reunion, some elderly folk, who were young in the early days when we were young, their grown-up children and their grandchildren. Some of the grown-up children Bill and I had delivered. I was talking to one of these middle-aged women who said she had been exploring that day at the site of the old log house. She found the remains of the picket fence which her father had built and the sweet williams her mother had planted were growing beside the fence. She said it was a heart-warming sight to see. "Heart-warming?" I said. "I would have thought that it would be heart-breaking." "Why, no", she said in surprise. "That life is finished. It was a hard life, but a happy one, but that chapter is over and we moved on to something else. I still have happy thoughts of our life here and it was a heart-warming experience to remember the old days when I was a child. The fence and flowers brought it back very vividly."

The summer of 1980 was the scene of another homecoming at Reesor. A memorial stone had been erected at the cemetery, which was dedicated in August. It stands as a memorial garden which John has landscaped. He has planted a tree for each person in the cemetery and laid out flower beds, a labour of love which will be a place of beauty.

THE DOCTOR TAKES A WIFE

6.

In one of Bill's letters to me in late summer he said, "I don't know what to wear for our wedding. Would a blue suit, black shoes and a moustache do? Do you want a moustache or shall I shave it off?" At the end of the letter - "<u>Please</u> tell me what to do with the moustache!!" (In the wedding pictures, the moustache was much in evidence.)

After a great deal of written debate, the wedding date was fixed for September 24th, 1931 at Bill's home in Glengarry, a double wedding with Bill's older sister Kate and her fiancé. My father, Dr. G. Watt Smith, officiated at the ceremony.

We spent our honeymoon in Quebec after which we returned to Bill's home in Glengarry for a few days. We left by train for Hearst in the first week in October, going via Sault Ste. Marie where Bill spent most of a day of our honeymoon discussing with a Sanitary Engineer the possibility of installing sewers in Hearst. On the last day of our journey a funny, (to Bill embarrassing), incident occurred. He had a pass on the railway and had assumed that his new wife would be included. This was not so. It was sometime later that the necessary forms were completed for me to receive a pass. It required most of Bill's ready cash to purchase a ticket for me which meant there was no money to buy meals on the train, a journey of a night and a day. About noon during a casual clearing out of his pockets in order to discard obsolete papers, Bill discovered a letter from a friend which contained a five dollar bill, in payment of a debt. Eureka! Off we went to the dining car.

We arrived at Hearst by the eleven p.m. train and spent our first night at the Waverly Hotel. This was prior to the days of private bathrooms in hotel rooms. The bathroom at the Waverly was down the corridor, with a china 'jerry' under the bed for close calls. As I sat on it before getting into bed it cracked loudly, to the amusement of my new husband and the embarrassment of his bride. The following day I was carried over the threshold of our first home.

The first year we lived in a furnished rented house, quite a comfortable one, but it had no indoor plumbing.

We carried our drinking water from the well and melted
snow in a big wash tub on the stove for washing and
everything else except drinking.

Early in 1932, which was the next summer, Bill said,
"Let's build a house." I was horrified. I was the
daughter of the manse where we never had much money to
spare and my father abhorred going into debt. Bill's
upbringing was different. On a farm, bank loans are
almost a necessity, to procure machinery, livestock etc.
So our attitudes to money were poles apart. It took me
several years to lose my worry about being in debt. I
said, "Bill, we can't! We have no money!" He said, "I
know, but we're earning every day. The bank will give
us a loan." It took a good deal of persuasion before I
consented and even then I had grave doubts but we went
ahead and I never regretted it. We were able to secure
a lot nearby that was large enough for a house and a
stable, there being no bylaw in the town forbidding the
keeping of farm animals. Bill had only been away from
cows during his college years and at the Civic Hospital,
so it was a very short time until we acquired a cow.
There was ample room in the stable for two horses also.
The house was started from plans we chose ourselves. It
was a nice house - square frame with three storeys,
four bedrooms upstairs. The house was heated with a wood
furnace and was a very comfortable home. A separate side
entrance led into an office and dispensary. When we
moved in we gave up Dr. Cain's office in the theatre
building.

Our first baby, Mary, was born August 7th, 1932
in our rented house. At that time it was a matter of
choice whether one was confined at home or at the
hospital. It had not yet become the practice for practically all deliveries to take place in hospital. We
had arranged to have one of the hospital staff nurses.
When we needed her Bill was unable to contact either
the doctor or the nurse because the operator at the
switchboard had fallen asleep. There was one night
operator and it frequently happened that she slept on
the job, so Bill had to go over to the hospital, pick up
the nurse and then go over to the doctor's house and tell
him that labour had started. We moved into our new
house with the baby before the house was really finished.
Her sleep during those first weeks was accompanied by
hammering which never seemed to disturb or bother her in

First Home
- 1931 -

Margaret and Bill
in front of the
hospital

New Home and Office
- 1932 -

Arkinstall Home 48 years later

any way. Bill's ready reply to people's congratulations
was - "My highest ambition now is to be a grandfather"
- with the certainty as with all young people that ful-
fillment was an eternity away. The years passed as if
on wings. Bill lived to achieve his ambition sixteen
times.

We had very little furniture. Our first 'chesterfield' was a long box covered with a wedding present
blanket, placed against the wall with cushions at the
back. We needed a table and chairs for the dining room
and Bill went to Brisson's furniture store to choose
them. He picked out a rather cheap set but Mr. Brisson
refused to sell them to him. "That isn't good enough
for a doctor", said he. "I'll show you what you should
have." He led Bill to a handsome walnut set with chairs
with leather seats. "You can have these at a reduced
price and you can pay me later." So Bill ordered them
and they looked lovely in our new dining room. The set
is still beautiful, the leather in the chairs shows
very little sign of wear fifty years later.

Mr. Brisson was an interesting man, clever, intelligent, fun-loving, and the town mayor for a time.
He had one weakness. He was too fond of alcohol and was
frequently inebriated. When he was in this condition
his sense of humour came to the fore. One evening he
arrived at the hospital after visiting hours, walked in
and was on his way up the steps when he was met by the
nurse on night duty, tall and dignified in her freshly
starched uniform, looking as if she had stepped out of a
band box. She told Mr. Brisson sternly that he could not
come in, whereupon he made a courteous, low, deliberate
bow, holding out to her with both hands the box of chocolates he had intended for the patient he was on his way
to visit. The nurse was so taken aback, she accepted the
chocolates and before she had regained her composure
Mr. Brisson was on his way down the corridor to the ward.
Bill happened to be in the hospital and arrived on the
scene while the nurse was still holding the chocolates.
She said to him, "What shall I do with these?" "Why,"
said Bill, "go and thank the gentleman, of course!"

Mr. Brisson had a pet bear he had raised from a cub
which he would regularly take out on a leash down the
main street. One day as they came to a street where
there was a stop sign the bear was straining at the leash
almost pulling his owner along, whereupon Mr. Brisson

called out sternly, "Where do you think you're going? Can't you read?"

The depression was at its height when we began our life in Hearst and it was not long before we began to see the line-ups that characterized these years, long line-ups for work of some kind, any kind. There were line-ups for hand-outs, also. It was a sorry sight to see the worried faces of discouraged men, unaccustomed to begging, desperately wanting to work for a living. Many rode the rails on top of freight cars in the slim hope of finding work in another part of Canada. Almost every week one or more men came to our door asking for food. We began to suspect that there was a mark beside our house. We would see a man stop at the telephone pole, study it for a short time, then make a bee-line to our back door. Although we too examined the pole we were never able to discover the code. Some asked for a job when they had finished their meal. In those days there was always wood to chop, not too hard a task for the men. None were refused a meal, even those who did not work.

Many people were on what was called relief at the time, or welfare. There just wasn't any kind of employment to be obtained. Since there was so little money it was not long before a medical system was set up to care for these people. They all had to have a number and when they came to our office, we had to find out what their number was. Then we would fill out our cards at the end of the month and send them to a compiling point such as we do now for medicare. One day a little twelve-year-old Mennonite girl came into the office. As we had to do with all of our patients at that time, except the ones that we knew were still able to pay, we were required to say, "What is your number? What is your relief number?" I asked the little girl for her number. She straightened up, threw back her shoulders and said proudly, "Mennonites do not take relief!" This was true. Mennonites somehow managed to get along without taking relief and through all this hard period they remained independent.

When we began our work in 1931, the operating room was in the basement. All the patients after surgery had to be carried up the winding staircase by means of a stretcher. There was no recovery room such as exists in modern hospitals where the patient would be left until

he or she regained consciousness.

The town which began with a large contractor's office and two stores was continuing to grow rapidly. The government was encouraging settlers to move to the wonderful clay belt, and the pulp camps reopened in 1932, as Dr. Stone had predicted during Bill's meeting with him in Ottawa. It was obvious that more space was needed to accommodate all the patients who were now coming to be treated. The second extension was therefore added in 1932 when the maternity ward and case room were added and the operating room moved to the main floor. This addition was made possible through the gift of $2,000.00 by a woman in memory of her daughter. The W.M.S. provided the balance of the cost and at the same time installed a steam boiler, sterilizer and X-ray.

We had not been long in Hearst before we realized
that there were serious problems at the hospital. Miss
Donaldson, the superintendent, who had trained at the
Glasgow Royal Infirmary, gave orders to her staff, all
graduate nurses, like a major general. The girls bitterly resented this treatment; moreover, Miss Donaldson
was inefficient. Her technique was so unsterile that
her nurses were in a constant state of worry. So it
was an unhappy situation, with the staff all lined up
against the superintendent. Someone wrote to the W.M.S.
Board in Toronto describing what was taking place. The
Board investigated, with the result that Miss Donaldson
resigned at the end of 1932. Edna Brown became acting
superintendent while the W.M.S. was searching for the
right person to send to Hearst, someone with tact, good
judgment and an understanding of people, who would have
the ability to build up an efficient, satisfied staff.

Margaret (Gretta)
Mustard R.N.

The one they selected was
Gretta Mustard who had just completed four years at Gypsumville
in northern Manitoba where she had
done a fantastic piece of work in
this isolated town sixty miles
from the nearest doctor, not only
nursing and delivering babies,
but also engineering the building
of a small United Church. It was
a delight for me to learn that
Gretta was to be our new superintendent. We had been room-mates
while I was at college and Gretta
was studying at the United Church
Training School in Toronto.

From her diary - "It took
me one night and one day to get
here from Winnipeg and the night
was spent in a perfectly good
tourist sleeper, but the day was a
long long trip on the tail end of
a freight train. I didn't know
that was to be my mode of travel

so I wasn't even fortified by a lunch, but luckily there were two teachers on the train and they shared theirs with me.

I got into Hearst at five p.m. expecting to be met with the town band, I guess, and lo and behold there wasn't a soul to meet me. I looked around a few minutes and then took the taxi to the Hospital. There I explained my presence and was admitted. Miss Jean Alexander, who is a friend of mine and would have met me, was out in the country and was late getting in. So I was pretty blue that night and longing for Gypsumville and my friends.

But first days soon pass and one soon makes new friends, and this is such a busy, busy place that one hasn't much time to think of oneself. I was sent up here to take on a big task. This hospital is our largest Church Hospital and for many reasons has had a rather difficult time.

I did not find it easy at first, but I think I am beginning to get the place running as I want it from the kitchen basement to the attic in both home and hospital. The nurses and the nurses' home had to be the first considerations. They certainly needed a home made for them and a house mother to keep it nice and to mother them. That did not take me long as I am first of all a homemaker, and how the girls appreciated it."

To have Gretta as superintendent at the hospital was a joy. We were on holiday at Bill's home in Glengarry when she arrived, and somehow communications had broken down. Also one never knew when the west train would arrive, which helped to explain her 'unHearst-like' initial welcome. She and I had been casual friends in residence at Toronto, and in Hearst the friendship grew and flourished. Bill, Gretta and I were a congenial trio, working very close together in both hospital and church. Our home was open to her whenever she was able to come. She dearly loved and enjoyed our children.

All of us could vouch for Gretta's ability as a homemaker. The majority of the staff lived in the residence; a smaller number were local girls. The residence was in every respect a 'home'. Many were the good times that not only the staff but also the people in the community enjoyed in that residence,- parties, get togethers, lots of fun and laughter. The dining

Staff in dining room, served in
the style of gracious living.

Garden party on the lawn behind
the nurses' residence.

room table, where all the staff ate together was set with a linen tablecloth, pretty china and silver, making all the semblance of gracious living.

It was the duty of the nurses' aide on night duty to awaken the nurses in the residence for the day shift. One of the aides, a fun loving, mischievious character used a different means of doing this each day. One morning she would put an icicle down the victim's neck, the next she would pull all the bedclothes off, the next she would put an alarm clock just about to ring on the pillow, another day tickle their toes. She always escaped in plenty of time before the half-asleep nurse could catch her.

Gretta writes: "I am trying to grow a few winter plants and it is almost hopeless as the windows are so cold. We have it twenty below Fahrenheit already and lots of snow. I have sent to a friend in Toronto for the odd plant. I guess that is the only way to have any. I have a lovely yellow chrysanthemum here in the office as I write. I want to get the grounds land-scaped a bit this spring and I hope to make some impression on it. We have lots of land for a good garden at the back of the hospital."

It was not long before there was a splendid garden producing various kinds of vegetables. The root crops, - carrots, turnips and potatoes were especially productive. The success of the garden was largely due to Harry, the caretaker and handyman. Harry loved gardening, which took precedence over all his other duties. If he were needed to repair something within the hospital and did not respond to a call, one would invariably find him in the garden. There was one drawback to Harry's gardening prowess - he preferred flowers to vegetables. He soon had beautiful flower beds blooming at the front of the hospital, which he tended faithfully. The vegetable garden did not receive the same tender care - Harry had to be regularly reminded that it required hoeing. "Harry will only look after the vegetables that have flowers. He likes potatoes", remarked one of the nurses.

All year round, Harry kept the church supplied with flower arrangements. In the winter - November to April - he would select one of his flowering plants (for he loved these as much as his outdoor flowers), wrap it up and carry it to the church in time for the service.

He was not concerned as to where he secured the quilt.
If he could not find an old one in the basement he was
not above removing one from a bed. His plants <u>had</u> to
be protected against frost. One Sunday morning one of

the nurses came upon Harry tending his flowers in the
garden. She didn't say a word but Harry was covered
with confusion. (In those days the Sabbath was strictly
kept, especially in a mission hospital!) He said, "God
won't care. I'm sure God won't care." Evidently he
wasn't so sure of the nurse's tolerance.
      Harry grew in that northern town the most gorgeous
sweet peas we had ever seen. Two or three of the
nursing staff used a large bunch of them to decorate
the little church in the country for the wedding of one
of the nurse's aides, transforming the drab little
church into a place of beauty. A vivid memory of that
wedding was our embarrassment when a collection plate
was passed which nobody expected, and the quick, mad
scramble in the pew for change. The bride was embarrassed too, as apparently this was not customary.

The head of each W.M.S. institution was required to submit an annual report to headquarters. The following are quotations from some of Gretta's reports:

"I had been at St. Paul's Hospital only a few weeks when Dr. Arkinstall came in one day and said, "There is a woman ten miles out in the country with a very severe pneumonia. Can you spare me a nurse?" I couldn't spare one off the staff as we were very busy. Dr. Arkinstall said he couldn't move the woman in her present condition or at least until the weather moderated. It was forty degrees below zero Fahrenheit. I said I would go, and my staff would carry on for the two or three days until we could bring the patient in.

I packed a bag of things I would need, put on my warm clothes and drove out to a Czechoslovakian home. I found there a young mother whose new baby was only three days old. She had got up the day after he was born to do a washing and in the extreme cold had contracted pneumonia. She was in bed in all her native clothes with a huge feather tick over her; her temperature was 102°F. She welcomed my hospital gown, pneumonia jacket and cotton sheets, much to my surprise. She welcomed also my smattering of Central European language as she hadn't a word of English. I studied Ukrainian at Ethelbert, Manitoba and it has served me well in many tight corners. I got the big family dish pan out, bathed my patient and made her much more comfortable with a few simple procedures.
She was very grateful and I knew we would get along very happily.

The baby had been taken home by a neighbour woman who had a baby of her own and found it just as easy to feed two. The father was the cook for the family. There were two little boys of school age, nine and eleven, and wee Tony was three. This house, like so many of its neighbours, had one room in which to eat, sleep and live. At night there were six of us and three cats to sleep in the same room which contained only two beds. The husband and his three boys slept in one, my patient was in the other and I was given three chairs in a row to make my bed on, but a few days later a neighbour brought me a stretcher, which I appreciated very much.

I did not have any chance while there to sleep but I could lie down for a rest at times.

The young mother was very, very ill and the doctor and I used all the skill we had to try and save her for her young family. Dr. Arkinstall drove out the ten miles with horse and cutter every day. During the times when the patient slept I had to make things to eat. The only thing the husband could make was macaroni soup and coffee, so I found myself making meals, enough to keep us going. I found he had some cured pork and some vegetables and he got me eggs and milk and flour to bake with, so after that we fared pretty well. The neighbour women were good to help out but all had families to care for. They were interesting women; when I baked a cake or some tea biscuits they watched me and learned how. When they saw me knitting they wanted to learn. I taught them how to knit, sew and bake. I talked to them in their own language enough to make myself understood.

I used to laugh when we gathered to eat. The table was just big enough to hold two, the rest sat around the room on benches as close to the table as they could get. The little boys all wore kerchiefs on their heads, and the ones who went to school wore peaked caps over their kerchiefs and because they were taught at school to take their caps off in the house they removed the cap but not the kerchief. They certainly were a picturesque little group with the embroideries and their added Canadian clothes."

Bill and I arrived one day just at dinner time when Gretta was preparing the meal, consisting of chicken soup. It smelled delicious and we were glad to sit down and share it. As Gretta was serving our plates and asking our preference she would say, "Do you want a drum stick? Do you like a wing?" as she forked each one out of the pot. Then, "Do you like feet?" Out came a chicken leg and foot complete with claws!

"We thought for a few days the mother would get better but her other lung filled up and she grew gradually worse. My two or three days grew into ten and I was getting very tired as I had never had my clothes off all that time and had had practically no sleep. On the tenth day the weather moderated and Dr. Arkinstall, partly for my sake, gave the 'command' to bring the patient into the hospital. So we put a feather tick over

her and drove in. I will always remember those three
little boys left alone in the house. They had dread in
their young hearts - we were taking their mother away.
Would we bring her back? I almost knew then that we
would not, but I still hoped. *

When we got to the hospital my staff was still over
busy and after a few hours sleep I went on duty with Mrs.
Janaski again. It was not for long. She lived only
two days after reaching the hospital. I was so thankful
she was in hospital when she died as the crying, moaning
men, women and children around her from neighbours'
homes in her last hours would have been hard to bear.
There had been many sessions while I was there, try as
I would to keep the room empty. The husband stayed in
the hospital with his wife, and we had also brought in
the baby. And now he must in all his grief prepare for
burial. He had to have a rough coffin made by a carpenter, but there was nothing rough about it when we laid
the young woman in. It was beautifully draped with
native shawls and embroidered silks from their own dear
land. It was as beautiful to them as ours with all our
lovely flowers. And thus the neighbours bore her to the
church and saw her placed in her last resting place. I
hope their Christian faith went with them in their sorrow.
I hope they, like the Israelites, did not feel that they
had left God in their home land. But no, I think they
felt God very near all that trying two weeks in the
kindness and help we were able to give them.

My story does not end here in all its sadness. We
saw the father and boys often because we had the baby.
We said we would keep him until he had a good start and
until the father was able to find a temporary home for
him. We had him eight months and he grew to be a beautiful boy. The father was very, very grateful and feels
he can never thank us enough. Dr. Margaret Arkinstall
and I were out in the Czechoslovakian colony a few
months later making some calls and we went to see the
Janaski family. The little boys were keeping house so
well while the father was away from early until late,

---

* Penicillin had not yet been discovered. In those pre-antibiotic days,
  the essential element in the treatment of pneumonia was nursing care.
  A patient must not be moved and must never be subjected to extremes of
  temperature. It was an anxious time until the 'crisis' occurred,
  usually about ten days from the onset. At the 'crisis' the patient's
  condition changed dramatically, either for better or worse. - M.A.

cutting pulpwood. The boys kept house, made meals and
took wee Tony with them to school. We asked the young
school teacher how she managed and she said she put up
with him in the morning and in the afternoon he slept.
After school they carried him home, fired up a cold
house and were doing their lessons when we went in at
five in the afternoon. They were brave young boys of
only nine and eleven doing their bit.

Then a happy thing happened in the Janaski home.
Mrs. Janaski's sister consented to come out from the old
country to marry Mr. Janaski and be a mother to his four
wee boys. This all took time and money to accomplish
but she came. The boys loved her and the home was happy
again. Last August the doctor called for me again to
go out with him to their home to help bring another baby.
I gladly went, only to stay the day. This time the
young mother stayed in bed and let the neighbours do the
washing and work. The new baby was a girl and I, hoping
this would be so, had taken out a little set of pink
baby woollies. The wee soft woollies so kindly made by
women of our church made the young mother in a strange
new land very happy. When I was leaving, the father had
a pailful of fresh eggs for me to take home with me. It
was a gift to me from a very grateful heart.

I have heard in many a home out there in the Czechoslovakian colony how much the Janaski family appreciated
what we had done for them, but I never heard a word of
it directly from them. I knew every time I saw Mr.
Janaski, although he did not talk about it at all. May
God bless these families and help them feel at home in
Canada.

I try to go out to that colony at least once a year
and it has been interesting to watch them open up the
country to make farming land. The women work with the
men. It is very hard to teach them to keep house. They
prefer to work outside. Consequently their children have
been in hospital a great deal and we try to tell them
that in this country a woman stays in and takes care of
her children, but they don't see it. They strap the baby
on their backs, go out to work taking the other pre-
school children with them.

The Czechoslovakians are a friendly people and loyal
friends. That group will do anything for me. The whole
colony feel they know me and when any of them come to

the hospital they ask for the little 'Russian' nurse
in the office, but when my vocabulary runs out, they find
out I am only of Scottish descent. Living there among
them, getting to know them, their hopes and ambitions for
life in Canada, made me realize how lovely they are and
how much they need friends."

*   *   *   *

"Two weeks ago one of the nurses took an old man
who had been there for ages to the Ottawa Hospital for
the Infirm. He was mental and a great old 'card'. On
Monday we sent a T.B. child to Toronto with a friend of
mine who was going to the city. Every day brings its
own interests and perplexities. Today we delivered a
woman in the case room and the doctors went right from
there to the operating room to do an appendectomy. In
the middle of the operation the maternity patient
hemorrhaged, became comatose and was in critical condition. I had to go in - give the anesthetic for
surgery and let Dr. Margaret go and rescue the maternity
patient. However, both are O.K. tonight."

The nineteen miles of road between Opasatika and
Mattice was finally completed in 1930. At first it
was a clay road (often mud) which was gravelled later.

Opening of the road. Railway station at
Hearst in the background

This was the first time that one could drive all the
way from Hearst to Toronto. The road was rather narrow
and full of interest. Just beyond North Bay it traversed
the Temagami timber reserve, about ninety miles winding
through bush, known as the 'Ferguson Highway'. One
never knew what one would see around the next curve, a
bear, a deer or a moose. There were no buildings or
gas stations along the way; we were told that we must
register upon entering and leaving the forest so that
all travellers would be accounted for. However, on our

first trip we were not called upon to do this and con-
cluded that the practice must have been recently dis-
continued. At Smooth Rock Falls the highway went
straight through the pulp mill yard, and the first time
we wondered where we had lost our way, only to find out
that this was the right way. The next interesting spot
was at Fauquier where we crossed the Groundhog River by
ferry. Our first experience was late at night, in the
summer of 1933. We were on our way to Bill's home for
a holiday. We had been delayed upon leaving home with
an emergency call so that it was nearly midnight when
we reached the ferry. A thunder storm had come up
while we were en route, with torrential rain. We had
our year old baby with us and I was terrified lest we
would get stuck, although the baby slept peacefully
through the whole journey. The entrance to the ferry
was a steep, very muddy, slippery hill. It was pitch
dark, so that we could barely see the ferry boat which
had only a dim coal oil lamp in the window. We managed
to drive on to it whereupon it began to chug chug and we
could feel that we were moving. At the other side of
the river the chug chugging ceased and we drove up another steep, slippery hill to the highway. We had not
seen or heard a human being. It was most eerie, and
reminded me of crossing the legendary 'river *Styx'
We had determined to reach Cochrane that night and
did so, although it was a weary trip. We always
took two days to drive to Toronto or Glengarry in
those days. How different it is now! All the exciting,
interesting features are gone - a bridge instead of the
ferry, a wide paved highway, bypassing all the towns
and villages, making it much shorter. One can leave
home to-day in the early morning and arrive at Hearst
by the same evening, observing the speed limit and
stopping for two meals.
     Some of our modes of transportation were unique. I
have already referred to the motor car on the track
called a 'speeder'. We acquired a small second hand car
for summer driving. At that time the roads were not kept
open and nobody drove a car in the winter. We all put

     * a river of the underworld over which the
              dead are ferried on their way to Hades

them up on blocks and left them until spring. Travel on these roads in the winter was by horse and cutter. Bill had a famous horse called Dick, famous because he was really an outlaw. He had been brought in from the west where he had been teased by cowboys, teased to the extent that he was an unsafe horse, really vicious. He mistrusted all men and would kick in such a way that he practically always made a sure hit.

The story was that in his previous home in western Canada a cowboy who wanted to buy the horse was refused by the owner. Thereupon the cowboy said to himself "O.K. If you won't sell him to me I'll make !%&#* sure nobody will ever ride him! To wreak his revenge the man and his friends teased the poor animal unmercifully, tied him in a stall with no head freedom, hit him with chains etc. until they had converted him into a vicious animal who tried to attack any man who came near him. He was later shipped to Hearst with a carload of horses and came into the possession of a friend of ours, an Ontario cowboy, named Dick. Aware of Bill's knowledge and love of horses Dick invited Bill to come and inspect the new arrivals. He saw the outlaw and immediately realized what a fine horse he was. He was a thoroughbred, with all kinds of endurance and stamina. He said to Dick, "What do you want for this horse?" Dick said, "Fifteen dollars." Bill said, "I'll buy him." Bill brought him home and named him

Dick after his owner. Then came the task of breaking
him in. It was not an easy job because Dick did not
respond to love; he had been too badly treated and his
memory of the cruelty that had been dealt to him was too
vivid. One night when we were getting ready for bed,
Bill was kneeling by the side of the bed saying his
prayers. He knelt so long I began to wonder why he was
praying such a long time. Suddenly he raised his head
and said, "I know what I'll do with Dick. I'll get
him in the deep snow." I said, "Did the Lord tell you
to do this?" He said, "I guess so. Anyway, I think it
might work." This is exactly what he did. He got Dick
out in the deep snow up to the top of his legs where he
was quite helpless and could not jump out and this is
how he got the harness on the first time. It took a
great deal of skill, patience, and time before the
horse could be hitched up and taken on the road, but at
last this was accomplished. After that Bill had some
wonderful trips with Dick. He could then appreciate the
fine qualities he saw in the horse at the start. Many
a hard trip out in the country on a bitterly cold night
saw Dick bring Bill home by himself. He was absolutely
trustworthy and very clever on the road. Bill could be
dozing in the cutter with the buffalo robe around him
keeping as warm as he could, while Dick would pull out
at the side of the road almost into the snowdrift to
meet another vehicle and get back on the road again,
Bill scarcely waking up. The horse was still unsafe
around strange men, never having lost his fear and
suspicion. It was embarrassing when Bill went out into
the country on a call. The farmer would come out
expecting to look after the horse while Bill went in to
see the patient. Bill would have to say very firmly
and sometimes sharply to the farmer, "No, don't come
near the horse. He's not safe!" This, of course, was
humiliating to a farmer who worked around his own
horses and Bill never liked having to do it. Even
though Dick was so vicious with men, he was the gentlest
of creatures with animals. The dog could come up to
him and even walk between his legs. All the first
winter that we had him, the rooster slept with him and
I honestly believe that a child could have played between his legs - it was only men he hated so much. We
had Dick for two winters and then Bill felt that it was

Bombardier snowplane.   Margaret and Bill
                on skiis.

Snowshoes, a very necessary
piece of equipment for the
northern trapper

time to get rid of him, partly due to the repeated
embarrassment when he went on calls and partly because
of the danger that sooner or later Dick would hurt someone. When he decided to let him go, we had to put him
away, as his wild temperament rendered him unsafe to be
sold. It was a hard decision to make。 Bill could not
forget the many hard trips through which Dick had transported him during those two winters. He was very
grateful and it hurt him deeply that this splendid
animal had to be put down. The next horses we had were
a beautiful black team called Jerry and Bessie. These

two were much easier to handle because they had been
broken properly before Bill bought them. He was a born
horseman, loved horses and was very skillful with them.
He enjoyed nothing better than to look after and drive
them.
        Later, in the early 1940's, Bombardier snowplanes,
run by propeller, were introduced. These held three to
four passengers. Winter travelling in a snowplane was
luxurious compared to riding in a horse drawn cutter,
to say nothing of the greater ease of transporting
patients from home to hospital。
        The train crew were informal, friendly men and Bill
knew them well. He was the C.N.R. doctor, held a permanent pass and he could get one for me each time I was
planning a trip. The train between Hearst and Nakina,
a mixed freight with one passenger car, running twice
weekly, had an erratic schedule, especially in the
summer during berry season. It would often stop for
half to one hour near a plentiful patch of raspberries
or blueberries, to let the passengers off to pick berries.
        When Mary was a baby I set off with her to my
parents' home in the province of Quebec for a holiday.
Bill was to follow later. We were at the station in
plenty of time for the 6:15 a.m。 train on a beautiful

summer morning. Bill checked the baggage, got us settled in the coach and drove home as the train pulled out.

Just as I saw the conductor coming down the aisle to collect the tickets I realized with dismay that Bill had not handed back my pass when he had gone into the station to check the bags; in our preoccupation of getting settled and saying goodbye (our first separation since we were married), we had both forgotten. I explained my predicament to the conductor, who told me not to worry, that he would telephone from the first station. Our little maid took the phone call, and ran out with the message to Bill, who was playing tennis near the house. He lost no time jumping in the car, and chased the train down the road at breakneck speed. I was watching anxiously from the window, as was the conductor, but he was less concerned. About twenty-five to thirty miles from Hearst, between stations, I saw Bill stop the car, jump out and wave frantically at the train. The conductor pulled the cord, the train stopped, Bill hopped the fence, scrambled across a field and gave the pass to the conductor waiting on the step.

A few years later one of our nurses and her husband were coming through on the train on their honeymoon. Bill had planned to be at the Hearst station to greet them but had been called away and was too late. Determined to see the bride, he chased the train, caught it at another station just as the conductor had called "All aboard!" Bill cried out, "Hold it! It's an emergency!" Whereupon he jumped on the train, found the honeymoon couple, kissed the bride, jumped off to the platform, calling out to the astonished conductor, "You can go now. I _had_ to kiss the bride!"

DOUG

10.

One of our dearest friends in the north, who
became almost a part of our family circle, was a
Scottish trapper named Doug Mitchell, a true pioneer.
Doug moved up into northern Ontario in the early days
and ran a trap line south of Hearst. It was one hundred miles in extent. He had what he called his main
camp in a picturesque spot beside a lake. In addition
were dug-outs as one friend called them, small shelters
at intervals of ten miles extending the length of his
trap line. Doug would stock these shelters with wood
and provisions in the summer and fall ready for the
trapping season when it began in early winter. His
main camp was a comfortable house with all the
facilities that one would enjoy in town, including
indoor plumbing, electric light, a radio, and an
electrically run washing machine. The electricity was
generated from a Delco plant which Doug had installed.
He even ate with sterling silver cutlery, inherited
from his mother.

The washing machine, however, was incapable of
overcoming human incompetence. Doug owned all-wool
Viyella shirts which he placed in the machine with very
hot water. He would examine them every so often and
if the cuffs and neck were not clean enough to satisfy
him he would add more soap and restart the machine.
Result - badly shrunk shirts. Our girls acquired
several of these, a good fit and beautifully warm.
Each time Doug arrived at our house with one of these
shirts he was subjected to a lecture on laundering
which eventually sunk in, with the result that the
girls did not get any more shirts.

His pioneer house was set in the bush several miles
from the railroad track, many miles from the nearest
neighbour, absolutely isolated and very beautiful. Doug
loved to entertain visitors. Bill would go regularly
in the fall during hunting season and he and Doug spent
many happy hours and days together. The attraction
for Bill was not so much hunting, although he did bring
back quite a few ducks on occasions, but the chance to
get away and have a good holiday and quiet time with a
very valued and true friend. They discussed all kinds

of things. Doug was intelligent, well read, kept up
with the times and current events and he and Bill had
many stimulating conversations, often far into the
night. Doug loved nature and nothing pleased him more
than to have people go to his house and appreciate the
beauty of his world, - his lake, the trees and wildlife - all the things that he so dearly loved.

The way to get to Doug's house was to take the
train south of Hearst and get off at a telephone post
that had a mile marker on it. Doug, of course, would
know ahead that we were coming and would be there with
his canoe. When we disembarked from the train, Doug
would be waiting.

We would load what we had brought, luggage, food
etc. into the canoe. The first few miles we would
travel a very narrow creek, so narrow that one could
put out one's arms and touch the trees on either side.
After a few miles along the creek, it opened up into a
wide lake, Doug's lake. The canoe crossed this until
we came to his cabin in the bush. It consisted of one
very large room, but when Doug had ladies visiting him,
he hung blankets across the room to make a bedroom for
them. He was very careful and particular to always pro-
tect our privacy and spare us any embarrassment. Never
did he take one woman to his house alone, always insist-
ing on having at least two.

Sometimes it was impossible to land the canoe on
dry land and in order to save his lady visitors from
getting their feet wet Doug, wearing his hip high boots,
would carry us one by one from the canoe to where there
was good footing on the shore. He was tall and strong
and we felt perfectly safe in his arms.

During our visits we would spend our days canoeing
along the lake, just enjoying the outdoors and the
beauty of the surroundings. Doug remained a bachelor all
his days. He loved the trapper's life. He knew that
rare indeed would be the wife who would settle in this
life style, especially when he would have to be away for
ten days at a time along his trapline. I suppose if he
had found someone for whom he cared enough to marry he
would have had to decide between a wife and the life in
the bush that he loved so much. Once he told us that he
had been trying to decide whether to get a wife or a
washing machine. He realized that he needed both but

Doug and young Mary
Arkinstall walking on
the railway track

'Sir Walter Raleigh' in hip boots assisting his
lady guests out of the canoe

decided in favour of the washing machine, equally useful and easier to get along with.

Doug was nutrition conscious and his diet was an adequate one. His culinary art, however, left something to be desired. One day his dish cloth mysteriously disappeared and after searching the cabin for it, Doug tore up another rag for a new dish cloth. He was preparing stew for dinner which he stirred periodically. The meat was very tender except for one rather large piece which remained tough. Finally Doug decided to remove the large piece and either cut it up to tenderize it or throw it away. Lo and behold! The mystery of the missing dish cloth was solved. No amount of boiling would have made any impression on that piece.

Doug was like an uncle to our children when they were growing up. He would come to Hearst periodically by train to do his shopping and banking and our house became his stopping over place whenever he was in town. We rarely knew when he was coming and he left pyjamas, toothbrush, comb - whatever he would need for the night at our house. When we went out for an evening, the door was never locked and many a time when we came home we would find Doug there having a cup of tea. He was very tall, strong and handsome with a wonderful physique. Our son admired him tremendously. One day a friend said to Billy, "I suppose you're going to be as big as your Dad when you grow up." "No", said little Billy. "I'm going to be bigger than my Dad. I'm going to be as big as Doug."

After we moved to southern Ontario we missed Doug's visits and his friendship a great deal. We were saddened when we heard that he had undergone a very serious operation in Kapuskasing. He developed Parkinson's disease and he was unable to trap any more. His mode of travel was entirely by snowshoes and one winter he realized that for the first time he was having trouble snowshoeing. His legs simply would not respond as they had always done. The following winter he refused to admit to himself that his ability was diminishing. He postponed going to the bush and spent time in Hearst with a friend doing odd jobs, still telling himself that he would go back to trapping later, but he never did that winter. At last he had to admit that his trapping days were over, a heartbreaking thing for him. Soon after he came to this

realization he visited us in our home in Newmarket
and we begged him to make his home with us. At that
time Mary had three small babies, the twins and her
next child one year younger. Doug could have lived
with her and her husband and would have been a great
help with the babies. He was so independent that we
knew we would have to make it clear to him that he
would be a help and not in any way a burden. Even then
Doug refused although we knew he greatly appreciated
the offer. His place was in the north. He went back
there and stayed with a friend until he died soon
afterward. We were very sad; we had many precious
memories of the times we had spent with him in his
northland and it was hard to realize that this
happy association was gone forever.

UNFORGETTABLE PATIENTS

11.

Medical practice in those days was in some ways
different from what it is now. Since then many more
laboratory tests for the diagnosis of illness have been
discovered and perfected. We did have a laboratory at
the hospital and were able to perform some tests while
others had to be sent away to Toronto for the results.
The same was true of X-ray techniques.

There was no blood bank with the various types
labelled that we could call on at once when we needed to
give a transfusion. The procedure for administering
blood was as follows: We had to type the patient needing
blood and find a donor of the same type. We called first
on relatives who would come to the hospital for typing.
If we were not able to find the type that matched, we
had to try elsewhere, perhaps the hospital staff, perhaps friends. When we did discover a suitable donor
after careful typing, the patient lay on the operating
table and the donor on a stretcher beside the patient.
Then we withdrew the blood from the donor and gave it
directly to the patient.

Antibiotics were unknown at that time. I shall
never forget when we first heard about penicillin, the
wonder drug as it was called. The first antibiotic we
were able to use was sulfa drug and later came penicillin.
Previous to the discovery of antibiotics the treatment
of streptococcus infections was continuous hot compresses
to the affected part and streptococcus serum which we
obtained from Connaught Labs in Toronto.

*   *   *   *   *

During the fourteen years at Hearst we treated a
good many patients. Some patients stand out in my
memory very vividly. There was a little girl with a
spina bifida. This is a congenital malformation of the
spine, characterized by an opening in the bony part of
the spine, causing the nerve supply to be cut off from
this part to the lower part of the body. At that time
surgery performed on this type of patient was done with
very limited success. Bill was able to operate on the
baby with an excellent result. The little girl grew up

to be perfectly normal and was able to walk and run like
any other child. Needless to say, a case of this kind
brings tremendous satisfaction and reward. His pay from
the family was - a pail of raspberries.

*　*　*　*　*

There was a woman who had been drinking one night
and during a fight, pushed her right hand through a glass
window. She was brought into the hospital late at night
with numerous severed tendons and bleeding profusely.
The hand was in such condition that probably a less ambitious surgeon would have considered amputation as the
only treatment. Bill called me to give the anesthetic
and we worked all night. It meant finding the ends of
each tendon that matched each other and suturing them
together, a very tedious procedure. It was daylight
when we finished and we all waited anxiously the next
few days to see whether the wounds would heal satis-
factorily without infection. The hand was immobilized
in a cast for a time and what a joy it was to find, when
it was safe to allow the patient to try to move her
fingers, that she was able to do so. Bill said several
times afterwards that he would love to see that girl
again to find out whether, indeed, the hand had regained
its normal use. She left Hearst and we were never able
to find her again.

*　*　*　*　*

There was a baby who developed a hydrocephalus,
water on the brain, very soon after birth, following
a very difficult delivery. The head increased very
rapidly and the baby became severely dehydrated. We
were unable to relieve the condition in any way and
from the length of time during which there had been so
much pressure on the brain, we all believed the little
boy would be severely retarded if he lived. We felt it
was a kinder thing to let him die but the father begged
us to do all we could to keep him alive. He said he had
faith that his little boy would become normal in spite
of all the signs that belied it.

A small infant cannot survive severe dehydration
for more than a short time, and special nurses were

assigned to the little patient round the clock to try to administer fluids. Intravenous treatment was practically impossible, which left feeding by mouth the only source. This was done with a medicine dropper at frequent intervals. Meanwhile the baby's head increased in size daily and I am afraid we did not share the faith of the father. Suddenly, what appeared like a miracle, occurred - the size of the head began to steadily decrease. In order to relieve the dehydration, Nature (God) had removed the obstruction between the brain and the spinal cord, allowing the excess fluid to permeate the body. From that time on the baby's progress was dramatic; soon the head resumed almost normal size. Our predictions that the brain would never function normally were unfounded. The child's mental and physical development were retarded, but with the loving care and attention of his parents, (the mother a trained and very clever teacher) their little boy caught up to the skills of his peers by the time he was six years old. He is a fine young man, holds a steady job and has always had a particularly loving, affectionate nature.

*　*　*　*　*

There was no highway south of Hearst, the only means of transportation being a track car or train which ran three times a week. It frequently happened that a pregnant woman who was at or near term, afraid lest labour should begin between trains, would develop pains in time to catch the train, be admitted to hospital, whereupon her pains would cease. Sometimes her stay in hospital would lengthen into weeks. When there was a suggestion that the patient might return home to wait there, invariably labour pains would recur, often to subside when the train had pulled out. False labour is a common occurrence and is very real to the patient. We were hesitant to discharge a patient as ten chances to one labour would have progressed at a time when there was no train.

These sojourns were pleasant holidays for the women, a welcome change from the isolation of their homes in the bush. They were very willing to do what they could to assist the staff, dusting the furniture in the ward, wiping bedside tables, feeding and entertaining the children, mending, sewing etc. Now-a-days they would probably have spent their time watching television. The longest stay on record was a month. This was a very obese woman who was admitted with pains that turned out to be false labour. The days passed with nothing happening. At last, after almost a month, Gretta said to her doctor, (our colleague, Dr. Aubin) "How much longer before Mrs. ------ will be confined?" The doctor who had a droll sense of humour, replied, "How could I feel anything through that cushion?" One day the women in the ward were measuring each other to compare waist sizes - the sixty inch tape would not meet around this woman! At last she began to have a normal menstrual period, whereupon the doctor examined her and discovered there was no pregnancy. This condition, in which the patient, usually at or near the menopause, has all the symptoms of pregnancy is relatively common. It is known as pseudocyesis. It is terribly difficult to persuade a woman in this state that she is not pregnant. This poor woman was, of course, discharged as soon as the diagnosis was made. She cried bitterly with disappointment and embarrassment. How could she ever break the news to her family and neighbours?

I had a similar case one night. I was called to a patient in her early fifties whom I had not previously seen, who was supposed to be in labour. As there was no road I had to hire a man to drive me on his 'speeder', a very cold mode of travel. When I arrived and examined the woman I had to tell her she was not pregnant. At first she was incredulous, then relieved (her only child was grown up and married), then embarrassed.

* * * * *

Jean, a little nine year old, was very ill with a generalized streptoccocic infection. We had fought hard for many days to save her, but in spite of all we could do, it seemed as if we had lost the battle. The hospital staff and our whole closely knit church family were saddened at the thought of losing little Jean, and many were the prayers that were offered for her. We had done all we could; the little girl lay in a coma, and the night came which we thought would be her last. She was in a private ward. Her special nurse, after making the little patient as comfortable as possible, was sitting beside

her, anxiously watching for any change in her condition.
Suddenly Jean sat bolt upright and stretched out both
arms. Amazing! She had been unable to lift a hand or
an arm for days, let alone sit up. Her eyes were wide
open, fixed on the wall at the end of the bed. As the
nurse gazed in astonishment, she saw Jean's face trans-
figured, her eyes shining, as she cried out clearly,
"Jesus! I am ready. Come for me!" The vision passed
as quickly as it had come, and the little girl fell
back on the bed. Now, she appeared to be sleeping
naturally. As the nurse continued her vigil, ponder-
ing the strange thing she had seen, she could see a
change in her little patient, and sure enough, in the
morning there were definite signs of improvement. Her
temperature had dropped slightly, she was conscious
and recognized people. Her recovery was slow, but at
last Jean became perfectly well, the only after effect
being partial loss of movement in an elbow joint. One
can imagine Jesus' reply that memorable night, "Not yet,
my child. I have work for you to do on earth." Jean has
served her Master faithfully ever since. She is an
accomplished musician, a choir director, a leader in
her church and community. She has raised a fine family,
now grown up.

* * * * *

Our second baby was born January 24th, 1935, the
coldest night of any, during all the time we were in
Hearst, sixty-four degrees below zero Fahrenheit. She
was born at home. Bill said he burned a whole cord of
wood that night, which was probably true. A few days
before Margie was born, we had one of the three day snow
storms which we seemed to have at least once every
winter. The first day it would snow, the second day or
day and a half it would blow hard, then would settle
down. It was very cold, the sun would come out and
the fresh fallen snow would sparkle like diamonds. It
was a Saturday night, Bill had to go to one of the pulp
camps on one of his regular trips and was unable to get
back because of the storm. His mother was staying with
us because I was expecting our baby any time. There was
a call late at night, a maternity patient two miles out
in the country who had elected to stay at home rather

than come into hospital. Had Bill been at home, he
would have gone, even though she was my patient but
as he was away I said I would go. We had a young man
boarding with us who was our 'chore boy', looked after
the horse, milked the cow, fed the chickens, did most of
the gardening in the summer and was a very all 'round
handy man. I called John that night and said that I had
to go out to the country. He hitched up the black
horses and drove me out. I sent him home again because,
of course, I knew I would be at the house quite some
time. I sat beside my patient and waited. The longer
I sat, the milder and less frequent the pains came until
at last they seemed to stop altogether. I realized then
that this was false labour. It was very late, my patient
was in a nice double bed so I got into the other side of
the bed and had a very good sleep. My mother-in-law at
home slept very little, worrying about me out there in
the country - my time for delivery so close. The next
morning the wind had stopped and it was a beautiful
sight, the sun shining so brightly on the freshly fallen
snow. As I try to recall that night and the next
morning, I cannot remember anybody else being in the
house; I don't remember the husband being there. It seems
as if my patient and I were the only ones. When labour
set in, we were to send for the neighbour next door. In
the morning, as there was no telephone in the house, we
had to hail a boy from nearby to go to the nearest phone
and call John to come and pick me up. That was Sunday
and my baby was born the next Wednesday. My patient's
baby was born a few days later, in the hospital rather
than at home.

* * * * *

There were times during our medical practice in
Hearst when aid was accepted and appreciated regardless
of the helper's station in life. In frontier towns
prostitution is common and Hearst was no exception. Too
often we judge and condemn these women as outcasts without taking the trouble to remember that they too are
human beings with hopes and dreams; having been born
into families with parents, brothers and sisters, they
love and hate, meet the daily problems of life in various
ways, want to be appreciated and loved, need friendship

just like the rest of the human race. Bill said of them
that they were the most loyal backers one could have.
One cold winter night while at the hospital, he had a
call to go out to the country to a very sick baby. It
meant going with the horse and cutter to bring the baby
to the hospital. It was a home where the husband was
absent at a pulp camp and there were other children in
the family whom the mother could not leave. Bill needed
someone to hold the baby while he drove the horse. He
wondered if a nurse could be spared but that night the
hospital was short staffed and it was impossible for anyone to leave. It happened that a young woman whom Bill
had treated for a veneral disease, a well known prostitute
was visiting in the hospital and overheard the conversation. She stepped forward and asked, "Could I help
you?" Bill accepted her offer with relief, sent her
home for warm clothes while he went home for the horse.
The woman was gentle, kind and understanding of the baby's
mother as she tried to waylay her worry. The tender
skillful way she handled the little patient on the trip
to the hospital was outstanding and Bill never forgot
it. On another occasion at a confinement in a home when
a woman was badly needed to help, it was an 'outcast'
again who came to the rescue and nobody could have done
a better job. The common concept of a hardened individual with thought for nothing but her own gain is
simply not true. These women proved they had a great
capacity for kindness, love and loyalty. What a tragedy
that they have been driven to such a perverted life!

AUNTIE

12.

Amid the joys and satisfactions of medical
practice I suppose every doctor can recall tragedies
when he loses a patient. We are haunted by the memories
of such a failure. Could we have done things differently,
or could someone else have saved the patient? In our
situation in those days there was nobody else to consult.
One of our failures involved a young woman who lived
next door to our house. She had a little girl of two
and a half years whom she had brought to our office to
be weighed regularly every month until the child was
too big for the baby scales. The mother, who was seven
months pregnant, suddenly began to bleed profusely. We
diagnosed placenta praevia, and rushed her to hospital
but in spite of all our efforts were unable to save her
life. To lose a mother and baby is probably the worst
thing that can happen to a doctor. It is a wonderful
thing that God is so powerful that He can cause good to
come from the worst of tragedies and this tragedy was
destined to have a very intimate impact on our own lives
in years to come.

The young woman's mother left her own home a block
away and moved in with her son-in-law and grand-daughter,
Gordon and Shirley Bates. Although she did her best, she
was a poor housekeeper and Gordon became increasingly
unhappy with the situation. His only sister, Chris,
lived in England, a trained nursery nurse, employed by
wealthy families. She had been with one family for eight
years and when their children had grown old enough to
go to boarding school Chris's services as their nursery
nurse were no longer required. Reading between the lines
in the letters she received from her brother during the
months and years it became more and more evident to her
that Shirley needed someone who would take her mother's
place more than the grandmother seemed able to do.
Chris's own mother had died when she was born. She had
been raised by an aunt and had spent most of her early
years at boarding school. She knew what it was like to
be lonely and long for a mother's love and wanted to
spare Shirley the unhappiness that had often been her
lot. She felt that her place was in Canada with her
brother and niece and it seemed that this was the

opportune time to leave her place of employment in England. When she announced her intention of leaving, her employer, a very dear friend, found numerous reasons why Chris should stay. She had endeared herself to that family so much that the lady of the house used all her powers of persuasion to keep Chris there, even though her role as nursery nurse was now redundant. At last Chris booked passage on a ship, not telling her employer friend until after this had been done. The parting was painful; Chris dearly loved this family, and she was leaving a familiar life to assume a new role in a strange land.

She arrived in Canada in March 1935, after a very rough voyage, a true pioneer. The sidewalks in Hearst were not ploughed in winter, the snow being allowed to pile up higher and higher until towards the end of

winter one was walking along at the same level as the fences. To a woman from England where there had been snowdrops and crocuses in bloom, daffodils and tulips showing leaves before she left, to be suddenly transported into what seemed to be a mid-winter scene was strange and unbelievable. Into what had she landed?

During her years of growing up she had never had to cook or keep house or to perform any of the household tasks a housekeeper would normally do. When she was eighteen she went straight from boarding school to training school into her nursery nurse course, after which she became employed in a wealthy household where she was a person of importance, with a maid to look after her needs, serve meals and do the necessary cleaning. It was, therefore, very difficult to come to

the little house in Hearst with no indoor plumbing, the
water for drinking to be carried from a well, and for
other purposes to be obtained from melting snow on top
of the stove. The day after Chris arrived she started
housecleaning and poor Gordon was carrying water all day
long. When he remonstrated with his sister for using
far too much, she replied indignantly, "How do you
expect me to get along with such a little? I haven't
used nearly as much as I would have for one bath at
home!" Chris had never before had experience with
managing a wood stove. It was all very new and very
frightening to her. Worst of all was Shirley's re-
action to her. Instead of the welcome which Chris expected, this auntie from across the sea, who had written
to the child and sent so many pretty things, Shirley
would not come near her, but shrank away in shyness.
"Why", Chris thought, "she actually seems frightened of
me!" This was indeed the case. When the grandmother
found out that Chris was coming she was terribly jealous
and brainwashed poor Shirley into believing her aunt
was a terrible ogre. "You'd better behave when your
aunt comes or she'll give you a licking." To this
gentle, kind woman who had received only love, affection
and trust from all the children she had looked after,
her own little niece's attitude was a rude shock. It
took time and much patience to overcome the damage
that had been done. It was all the more so because
Chris, realizing how much the grandmother would miss
Shirley, took the child to her grandmother's house each
afternoon to spend two or three hours with her.

With characteristic Hearst hospitality, Chris was
invited for tea to a number of houses. She wanted to
repay her hostesses and invite them back, but what would
she give them to eat? She had never made a cake in her
life and there was no English bake shop in Hearst. She
tried the recipes - sometimes with successful results
but more often not. She always gave herself time to
make two cakes, in case the first one should be a failure. She found that shortbread was the easiest thing
to make, more certain than a cake to turn out right.
There were no dainty cups in the house, such as her
neighbours had, no good table linen or silverware such
as Chris had been accustomed to all her adult life. She
went shopping for some of these things. There was a
kind, understanding clerk in the local hardware store

who was a wonderful help, advising her what to buy and assisting her with Canadian money. Living almost next door we, too, were able to help Chris in many ways to become oriented and adjusted to this different life.

Three year old Mary often ran across the street to visit Chris, who always welcomed her and took time to talk to the little girl. When we missed Mary we were fairly sure where she would be, and my young maid or I would run across to bring her home, there being no phone at the Bates'. This was happening so often that I thought the child would be a nuisance, so I told Mary she was not to go to visit "Miss Bates" unless she was invited. The next time Mary saw Chris she said, "My mother says I'm not to come to your house." Chris assured me of Mary's welcome at any time, that she filled a need in Chris's life just then, and begged me to let her come. We invented a signal - when Mary was there Chris would hang a red cloth from the window.

At this time my helper in the house was a young girl who did much of the cooking and housekeeping. When I resumed my practice after Margie's birth it was obvious that there would be too much work for one girl, now that there was a baby. Chris had become very attached to our children, the more so because they responded to her with trust, having none of the inhibitions that had been implanted in Shirley. Margie was born six weeks before Chris arrived, and she always said she and Margie came together. I asked her if she would consider coming to our house during my office hours every day and take charge of the children. She accepted with delight, and brought Shirley with her when she was not at the grandmother's. It was a wonderful boon to us and the beginning of a precious friendship. The children loved her dearly; she was 'Auntie' from the time they were old enough to talk.

CAMP ATHOL

13.

Ten miles north of Hearst is a lake called Lac Ste. Therese. This is the beginning of a chain of lakes which can be followed with portages all the way up to James Bay. On one of these lakes known as Pivabiska, Bill had a cabin built in the year 1935. This was unorganized territory and we purchased a sizeable piece of land with lake frontage for the incredible price of fifty cents an acre. The cabin, built of logs, was the scene of many happy times during the summers that we lived in Hearst. The carpenter was a Swedish man, Ed Larson, a very skillful, meticulous workman. Never have I seen a cabin that could compare to this one. The logs were fitted together so skillfully and so closely that there was no need for chinking such as one usually sees in a log building. The logs fitted absolutely tightly with no hint of even a tiny space in between. We had a holiday every summer at Camp Athol, so named after Athol in Glengarry County where Bill and I first met and where our homes were. Bill would stay as long as he could, a week, perhaps two weeks. The rest of us stayed usually for the whole month of August. We always went in August because at that time there were practically no mosquitoes or blackflies such as there were in June and July. Camp Athol was accessible only by boat. The first few years we had to leave from Lac Ste. Therese by motor boat, a journey of about eight miles. In later years there was a road built - a road of sorts - certainly not anything like a paved highway, but traversable with caution and care - which came to an end just opposite the cabin. The trip across the lake from there was only half a mile, making it much easier to reach the camp.

The year that we built the cabin Margie was seven months old and Mary was three years. The ladies camped in a tent, my sister-in-law, my sixteen year old niece, the children and myself. The carpenter, a young man helping to build, and Bill slept in a bark covered tee-pee. Our beds consisted of small spruce logs laid closely side by side, covered generously with spruce boughs with quilts on top. They made very comfortable soft beds. We put the baby by herself in a corner with a log

Bark covered Teepee (foreground) that the
men slept in, tent for the ladies in the
background. True pioneer campers in 1935,
roughing it while they built their log
cabin.

Camp Athol

covered with a quilt to simulate the side of a crib. We
thought it was a lot of fun even though it rained a
great deal. Looking back on it now, I question it. In
those days disposable diapers were practically unknown.
We used cloth diapers for the baby and it was no easy
task to get them dry because everything else was wet.
We would stand all together round the bonfire shaking
the diapers until they were dry. We cooked on an open
bonfire, camping in real pioneer fashion.

We did a great deal of fishing when the weather
would allow and fared sumptuously on fresh fish and bacon.
The cabin was completed and ready for occupancy by the
next August, all except the front verandah which was
added later, and every summer from that time we spent a
happy month camping. How we loved the cabin and the
lake! How wonderful it was to sit on a rock by the
water with a book, reading or just dreaming, enjoying
the lake with its lights and shadows constantly changing,
the spruce forest all around, the sunsets, - to listen
to the wind in the trees, squirrels chasing and scolding
each other and me, blue jays squawking their message that
they wanted something to eat. It was so peaceful, no
telephone to call us to work, no clock to order our days,
a perfect holiday.

Many good times we had there. In addition to our
own family holidays we opened the lodge to C.G.I.T.
and boys' groups. For six consecutive years we held
C.G.I.T. camps for a week to ten days. They were planned for the week just preceding our family's camping
time, very convenient for us as it meant no necessity to
put away boats, clear the cupboards of food etc. We
even came in for the C.G.I.T. left overs. I believe
camp programs have changed somewhat through the years,
but in those days we had a program suggested by the
National Camp Committee which I consider to be the
best possible as a meaningful, inspiring experience
for teen-agers. We could accommodate about twenty-
five, including four to six leaders. There were two
small bedrooms in which the leaders slept, the campers
sleeping on mattresses on the floor, ten on the screened
in verandah with mattresses laid side by side, and ten
in the upstairs room which was like an attic in which
one could stand upright only in the centre where the
roof came to a peak. The stairway up to the attic had

a banister and landing leading out from the room. This
made an ideal stage for plays. One of our favourites
was A.E. Milne's 'The King's Breakfast'. The banister
was just right for the king to slide down in the part
where he has gone back to bed sulking because there is
no butter for his bread. Then, in jubilation, when he
gets some butter - out come the king and slides down
the banister.

I look back with nostalgia to the daily Bible study
period. We gathered all together in a circle as soon as
the breakfast dishes and tidying were done, when we sang
the camp hymn suggested for that particular year. At
our first camp it was "Be Thou my Vision", a hymn which
had previously been unfamiliar to me. Ever since, whenever I have sung that hymn, I am back in the circle in
front of the cabin amongst twenty teenage girls, mothers
and grandmothers now. Emotion grips me, my voice chokes
and my eyes fill with tears. After the hymn we dispersed
into little groups, each with an adult leader, all of us
carrying our Bibles, to our chosen spot among the trees.
The Bible study course was laid out for us in the camp
guide so that all were studying the same passages of
scripture. In small groups of five or six the girls
spoke out freely. We had intimate, profound discus-
sions and the girls in those few days came to have a
personal relationship with God. After the Bible study
period we all gathered again, sitting on rocks, stumps
or grass, while one of the leaders gave us a short talk.
Then came free time and a rush for swimming, hiking or
whatever one chose.

I had never been to a C.G.I.T. camp. Indeed I had
never belonged to C.G.I.T. When I was a teenager the
organization was in its early stages and there was never
a group in any church to which I belonged. Genevieve
Carder, who was very experienced in Girls' work and
camping, generously called herself and myself co-direct-
ors, even though we were "expert" and "greenhorn". She
taught me such a great deal, I veritably believe I might
have been able to direct a camp on my own at the end of
those six years. One summer we had the Carder baby,
born in May, (this was the end of July). We had a crib
which had been built right in one of the rooms for our
own children, where little Billy slept peacefully. At
two and a half months this little boy had no qualms about
being in the midst of a C.G.I.T. camp. In fact, he

actually seemed to enjoy it. Several times our Sunday
worship was a 'Gallilean' service. There were two
large rocks jutting out from shore two hundred feet
apart. Half the girls would gather on each rock and
we began our service with "Jubilate", sung antiphonally
from rock to rock, after which the girls on the far
rock would walk through the woods still singing till
they took their places with their companions. The two
leaders who were conducting the service would push out
from shore, anchor the boat with a big rock tied to the
rope and address the 'congregation' from the boat.
Teenagers are very impressionable and many have spoken
through the years of how much camp meant to them.
     We had no close neighbours. As the only access was
by boat, visitors announced their approach by the sound
of their motor several minutes before they docked at
the wharf. After one C.G.I.T. camp, when all the girls
had left, bag and baggage, several of us leaders had
stayed behind to clean the cabin and make it tidy. It
was a hot day. We wanted a good wash after our work so
all of us made our way to the lake minus our bathing
suits. We had time for a good splash when we heard a
motor boat which sent us scurrying up the hill to the
cabin for some clothes. We got down to the dock to
greet our visitors just as the boat arrived, three
young men looking very amused. "What was the joke?" we
wondered. The answer was a set of binoculars on the
boat seat!
     The year we had the goats was a memorable one.
Never have we had so much fun with any of our animals
as with those two goats. On one of Bill's trips to the
country to see a patient, the farmer, when discussing
the bill said, "I haven't much money right now. Is
there anything around here you might be able to use?"
Bill spied the two goats, each one about to have a baby.
He thought of the long eight mile boat trip from the
cabin to the nearest store, figuring that the goats would
give fresh milk daily, so he said to the man, "How
about those goats?" Thereupon the deal was made. They
were giving plenty of milk by the time we were ready to
go to camp in August. They were easy to transport; we
simply put them in the back seat of the car, transferred
them to the open boat and got them easily to the cabin
with no problem whatsoever. They gave just enough milk

so that the trips to the store were cut down to a great
extent. The goats were very tame and loved company. At
first we intended to let them fend for themselves around
the cabin without being tied because goats will eat anything. But after a few days we gave this up because
everywhere we went the goats followed us, - down the
path to the little house in the woods, there being no
indoor plumbing in the cabin, - on the path to the well
which was also our refrigerator, - indeed everywhere we
went. If they thought we were not going quickly enough
we got a hefty reminder in the rear. There was a verandah
on the front of the cabin by then, and the goats could
push the door open without any problem. They would come
up the steps, push open the verandah door and peer in at
us through the window with their front hoofs on the sill.
It seemed whenever we looked out of the window there were
one or two heads peering at us. All this was rather dis-
concerting, so instead of letting the goats wander around
loose we decided that we would tie them up in various
parts to graze. When they finished grazing in one area
they were tethered in another place. At this time Mary,
who was about eleven years old, milked one goat and
Margie, age about nine, milked the other. One day Margie
was feeling sick, and didn't feel up to getting out of
bed to milk her goat. I said, "Never mind. I'll milk
your goat." Do you think that goat would let me milk
her? I tethered her outside the cabin as Margie always
did. She had to stand on a raised box to be high enough
for an adult to do the job. Perhaps this was why she
refused to have anything to do with me. She climbed up
the wall of the cabin, moved back and forth, did anything
that prevented me from milking her. She was just not
going to let this strange person have any milk, so in
the end Margie got up and milked her goat who stayed
perfectly quiet throughout the whole proceeding.

The children all learned to swim at Pivabiska as
we spent many hours each day in the water and at the
dock. They loved to fish and spent a great deal of time
in the boat on the lake trolling. We caught mostly pike
for which we did not care very much, and pickerel which
was delicious. One evening I was out in the boat with
our own four children and three others; we had been
trolling for quite some time without much success when
suddenly there was a tremendous tug on Mary's line. It

Milking the goats

Mary's fish - a Muskalonge,
nearly three feet long
weighing over eleven pounds.
Our record catch for all
our years of fishing and
delicious eating.

almost pulled her out of the boat. She reeled it in and presently we saw the largest fish I have ever seen. Its head was tremendous; it looked almost like a whale to the children, who were frightened and all crowded to one end of the boat while Mary was pulling in this huge fish. As it got closer its head and mouth looked bigger and more frightening. "How are we going to land such a monster?" I said to Mary. "Let it go! Let's cut the line!" "No," cried Mary. "I spent sixty cents for this line and I'm not going to let it go." As she was still hauling it in, the closer it got to the boat, the more scarey it looked to the children huddled at the end of the boat, some of them screaming. One of the children was so fearful that I refused to have the fish in the boat lest the child would panic and jump out. At the risk of losing this catch, we rowed for shore towing the fish, the hook tearing through its mouth and Mary screaming all the way to shore, "We're going to lose it!" On the shore I was able to kill it with a very hard pounding. It was a big fish, nearly three feet and weighed over eleven pounds. It was almost as big as Mary. It was a muskalonge and was delicious eating. That was our record catch for all our years of fishing.

We had one major accident up there. One morning Bill was carrying young two and a half year old Billy on his back. The board walk was slippery from the morning dew and Bill slipped and fell. In order to save little Billy, Bill came down hard on his back. It was evident that he had had a severe injury. He was unable to move without a great deal of pain and I suspected as Bill did that he had broken his spine. This turned out to be the case. We had a friend staying with us at the time who stayed with Bill and the children while I took the boat and went to the nearest telephone, eight miles away, to call the hospital for an ambulance. I waited and transported the ambulance attendants by boat across to the cabin. We loaded Bill on a stretcher and as carefully as possible took him in the open motor boat across the lake to where the ambulance was waiting. An x-ray confirmed our suspicions - there was a fracture of the middle part of his spine. As he himself was the only surgeon at that time who could have adequately treated this kind of fracture, he went to Toronto to the General Hospital. I went with him and he was treated by one of the orthopedic surgeons. He was put in a body cast and after a week and a half we were able to return home. The cast was very uncomfortable but he was able to get around and it was not long until he was carrying out his work almost as intensively as usual, even operating. The cast was supposed to remain in place for four months. It became so uncomfortable and itchy that one day after a particularly long stint in the operating room Bill was absolutely fed up and against orders, took matters into his own hands and proceeded to cut off the cast. He was not able to complete the procedure by himself but he had succeeded in ruining the cast to such an extent that there was no alternative but to have one of his assistant doctors complete the job. Fortunately there was no harm resulting from this and although he had a certain amount of discomfort for some time he made a very good recovery.

There were a lot of raspberries and blueberries near the cottage which were at their best in August during our camping time. I like to pick berries, so did it for pleasure; the children picked for duty, and all enjoyed these fresh wild berries many days while we were there.

We had many visitors. Wednesday was store closing time in Hearst and this was the day the people often went to the lake. Also, people frequently came from the other cottages to get water as we had the only good spring water that we knew of on the lake. There were two or three other cottages - not many at that time, and we would all gather at one cottage or another. It was common to have a group of twenty or twenty-five people around our table Wednesday or Sunday. These holidays at Athol Lodge were very precious. The best part was the time we were able to spend together as a family. There was no telephone to call us away, which gave us a perfect time of rest, relaxation and fun.

* * * * *

A Holiday in Ontario's Northland
- Gretta (Mustard) Crookes -
- 1950 -
"We were going back to the north from our homes in southern Ontario, to bask on the sunny shores of Lake Pivabiska for a month. Our husbands did not feel that

they could go so we had to go without them. We loaded
the trailer with good provisions from the Arkinstall
farm, apples, potatoes, vegetables, home cured and
canned meats, dozens of cookies and several loaves of
homemade bread and started blithely on our way. It was
my first time back since my marriage nine years before
so it was with keen anticipation that we set forth.

Our little group was made up of Margaret who drove
all the way, fourteen year old Billy who took over when
his mother got the trailer jack-knifed while trying to
back up, nine year old Jean, Chris Bates, our dear
friend, myself, my six year old Elizabeth and two wee
black kittens who were supposed to remain in a box but
visited everyone in the car. We planned to take as long
on the journey as we wanted, staying in cabins and
cooking our own meals. We had one breakdown en route,
the oil pan sprung a leak and much as Margaret hated
seeing people chewing gum like cows chewing their cud,
we were all encouraged to chew so that we could fill the
hole with gum until we got to a garage. After three
days we reached Hearst where we stayed with friends
overnight. We left Chris in town to visit with her
brother and we set out in the morning for Lake Pivabiska
and Athol Lodge. We loaded our provisions into
the boat, packing it carefully, leaving just enough
room for ourselves. Billy was our navigator, that day
and all the rest of the month, piloting us safely in
the little motor boat.

The first day meant setting up beds, cleaning up
mouse tracks, getting out food and settling in for the
night. Our kitties began their duties at once, but insisted that we appreciate their work and one kitty
carried her mouse up onto the bed where we were sleeping.
Margaret, being the braver, crept silently out of bed
with kitty by the neck whispering to it, "Hang on tight
to your mouse." The kitty obliged until both were safely
outside.

With no church to go to on Sunday we set up our
own Sunday School in a lovely shaded spot overlooking
the lake. Billy had brought his violin and accompanied
us as we sang. We read the psalms that David wrote in
just such surroundings. Most Sunday evenings friends
would come from Hearst to visit and these get-to-gethers
were wonderful. With the help of a huge bonfire and

plenty of good food we made merry with sing-songs and conversation. Sometimes we had a worship service with many of us participating. One evening I led in prayer thanking God for the Sabbath day and all its glory and at the end one lad said, "Did you forget it is pouring rain?" To that I pointed out that rain was a real blessing, too.

Washday was back breaking fun, using two large wash tubs set on stumps and lake water, anytime, not necessarily on Monday, not early in the morning, just when the spirit moved us or perhaps I should say when we ran out of clean clothes. We did nothing by the clock. Margaret was washing merrily at five p.m. when I served elevenses (the eleven o'clock in the morning cup of coffee).

Elizabeth found a toad one day and Jean, who knew all about nature's wildlife, helped fix a nice deep wide box lined with moss. They put a dish of water in it and caught flies and insects for him to banquet on. Toad seemed to love it but one day he got away and no amount of searching could find him. The children gave up and everyone went off for a boat ride leaving me (I am not a water person) happily baking bread. In the quiet cabin I was surprised to see Toad come out of some secret hiding place to join in the bread making. He lived with us for a week and then we persuaded the girls to let him join his playmates in his natural surroundings. With many goodbyes from the girls he hopped away.

One of our happy duties was picking wild raspberries. We never made work of it, picked only when we felt like it. Billy and a Hearst chum, Wayne, would pick any day for an extra pie. There were blueberries too, but not near the cabin. We had to go by boat to other places on the lake to find them.

A trip to Lake Fushimi had been planned for days. This was a large lake belonging to the chain of which Pivabiska was one. This chain of lakes emerged at James Bay. We started out in great spirits with lots of food, our bathing suits and warm clothing for coming home at night. We had been given intricate directions on how to wend our way through the narrow lakes, portages etc. but missed a turn somewhere and by noon were hopelessly lost. For two more hours we kept on where many times only strong arms pulled the boat through. We agreed to turn back to the open lake and start again but first we had a well earned lunch. We re-read the map and decided to try the only other water path. This was the right one and by four o'clock we were in sight of Fushimi. We had planned to spend a little time there swimming and picnicking but we knew we must turn back if we were to be home before dark. We had no light on the boat, not even a flashlight. Never had anyone done a better piece of work than our fourteen year old did that night as he guided our little motor boat with its precious cargo through strange waters safely home. As we crawled out of the boat, everyone was stiff, partly from fear and partly from sitting so still. No one had voiced it but we all had felt the danger and were grateful for the unseen Presence that had come with us all the way.

There are always accidents and excitement when camping. Our first was when Jean took her first dive. Her glasses came off and she came up without them. "Too bad", said Margaret. "Some of us will dive down and get them. We have often recovered things before." No amount of diving all that month produced the glasses and Jean had to carry on without them. Billy and Wayne were out in the boat when Billy lost his watch. "Too bad", said Margaret again. "I wish you hadn't been so careless." Of a more serious nature was the day Jean fell down the cliff in front of the cabin. It was no mean fall and those of us who witnessed it were really frightened. Margaret, though frightened too, was calm and collected and soon had her little daughter fixed up and comfortable and we all hoped there were no serious hurts. Next day she was all better and ready for more escapades. One night we got a call for help from a neighbour so Billy and Margaret with black bag in hand took the motor boat and went on a medical call. I was left alone with two little sleeping girls and let my imagination run wild thinking of all the things that could befall a lone woman in an unlocked cabin. However, by midnight Billy and Margaret were back and all was well.

The children all had their separate ambitions. Jean had learned to row and was able to take the boat out in the bay alone. Elizabeth had lost all fear of the water but did not quite learn to swim. Billy wanted to swim across the bay, half a mile. He had been getting into condition all month so towards the end of our stay he tried his swim, Margaret going along beside him with the row boat. He made it! This was a splendid achievement for him.

The month passed all too quickly and there were only three precious days left in camp. Our friend Doug arrive as we had hoped he would. How the children loved him! He brought treats of food and our table was laden with them. We had a canoe, but the children were forbidden to use it. When Doug arrived, an expert canoeist, we launched it and we all had rides with him. We acted the King's Breakfast for him and could not have wished for a more appreciative audience. He took the children on hikes, told them stories, and played with them tirelessly. He even scrubbed the cabin for us before we left and came into Hearst to see us off. He made our last three days doubly happy by his cheerful presence which lessened the sadness of leaving our beloved northland.

Before our final departure we visited those places that had been so dear to us, as many of the homes as possible, the inside of the United Church where we saw the pictures we had carefully purchased for the Sunday School, the curtains we had helped to make for the partioning of the classes, and the two large flags that I had placed in memory of my brother Thornton, lost from the Athenia. As we walked around the hospital and the nurses' home we recalled how much hard work we had put into it as we brought it up from a very small beginning to its capacity of sixty-five beds. The staff were all strangers and knew us not. We did not go inside, but I just had to take a peek in my old bedroom window before going quietly away. Our month was over and we left the northland behind us once more. When would we see it again?"

Gretta never did return to Hearst. We went to Hearst to the cabin only once after that. The time spent travelling was three days each way and to make the trip worth while one should spend at least three weeks there. The children were all growing up with friends at home, and with other summer activities were no longer interested in going so far away from home. So, regrettably, we decided to sell Athol Lodge, putting

Athol Lodge - 1979 -

it away with our other precious Hearst memories. Our place was in southern Ontario now and we soon realized that it was not the place that made the summer memorable; it was the friendship.

"Bay named for Newmarket Doctor"

"The name Arkinstall Bay will appear on official maps this year for the first time as a feature of Pivabiska Lake in the Cochrane District of northern Ontario.

It has been on unofficial maps of Hanlan Township for over forty years.

The name, which commemorates a pioneer Hearst-area physician, Dr. William Arkinstall, was approved recently by the Ontario Geographic Names Board and the Ontario Ministry of Natural Resources through the request of J.E. Hietala of Hearst and fifteen of his neighbours." (portion of an article taken from the Newmarket Era, Wednesday, September 19th, 1979.)

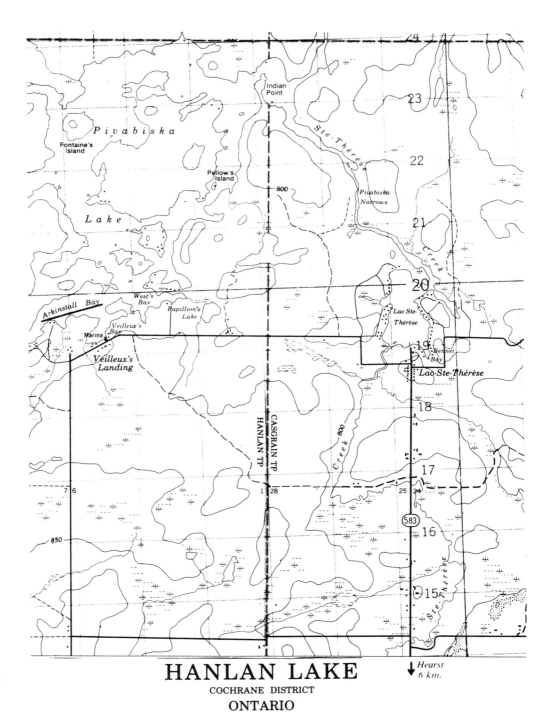

HANLAN LAKE
COCHRANE DISTRICT
ONTARIO

↓ *Hearst*
6 km.

87.

PARTIES AND FUN

14.

In those pre-television days we provided our own fun and entertainment, the church being the centre for get-togethers in the Protestant community. We had regular social evenings at which we would gather for entertainment, with refreshments at the end of the evening.

At one of our Hallowe'en Parties we enacted Blue Beard's Wives. We hung up a large sheet with seven slits in the sheet at about the height of a person. Seven women stuck their heads through these slits. Those of us that had long hair had it fastened above to the sheet. Those who had shorter hair wore wigs which were also fastened above. Mercurochrome was scattered generously below the sheet, and our faces were whitened with powder. As we took part in the tableau our eyes rolled upward and our mouths hung open looking as dead as we could play the part while Blue Beard brandished his sword.

* * * * *

At another masquerade party, Bill was late arriving, having had a case which delayed him. The judging was all completed and we were just about ready to serve lunch. In came Bill down the steps, making a very dramatic entrance riding a horse as Yankee Doodle Dandy. He had a hat on his head which I recognized at once as my very best 'go-to-meeting hat'! He had gone to the barn where the chickens were roosting and sleeping, pulled a feather out of one of the roosters, stuck it in my hat, put it on his head and came in riding the horse. The animal was constructed out of an oblong frame of wood, Bill standing in the middle of the frame. Make-believe legs hung down either side, a large grey blanket covering Bill's own legs. The head was made out of heavy cardboard or plywood, complete with reins which he held in his hands. He made a dramatic entrance, galloping down the stairs and all around the room as Yankee Doodle Dandy with the feather in his hat, my very best go-to-meeting hat!

At that same Hallowe'en party my costume was 'The Fine Lady Riding Upon a White Horse'. "Ride a Cock Horse to Banbury Cross to See a Fine Lady Upon a White Horse, Rings on her fingers and bells on her toes, she shall have music wherever she goes."

My horse was a large rocking horse that Bill made on one of the rare occasions when he was at home for a full day. He was recovering from an attack of the flu and was well enough to make the horse. The body was a  solid block of wood. He made legs fastened on the body and the rockers, and fashioned a very lifelike head. This horse stood almost four feet high, was very solidly constructed and could easily carry quite a big child. Our children had a lot of fun playing with it. In preparation for the Hallowe'en party I painted the horse white, I had an old fashioned white dress with plenty of jewelry and beads to go with it, went barefoot with little bells fastened on my toes, several rings on my finger and sat on the rocking horse, playing the part of the nursery rhyme.

The tail of the horse has a story connected with it. In those days our groceries were delivered in winter, not by truck, but by horse and sleigh. The man who made the delivery was very fond of his horse called 'Barney', a grey horse with a grey mane and tail. One day I said to Johnny, "I need a tail for my rocking horse. Could I have a piece of Barney's tail?" "No!" said Johnny indignantly. "How could I ever give you a piece of Barney' tail for a wooden horse?" "Oh, please, Johnny! He'd never miss just a few hairs off his tail." Again Johnny indignantly refused. The next time Johnny came to the house on a delivery, I had Chris, my very good friend, engage Johnny in conversation, taking his attention while I ran out with the scissors to where Barney was standing quietly as he always did, lifted up his tail, snipped off a sizeable bunch of horse hair and brought it in. It was not at all evident from the top and I knew that Johnny wouldn't notice anything missing. That

night I got Bill to fasten the bunch of horse hairs together with a piece of wire, I washed and dried them and
Bill attached the new tail to our wooden horse.   The
next time Johnny came on a delivery I said, "Johnny, I
got a tail for my horse. Do you want to see it?"
"Sure", said Johnny. "Where did you get the tail for
your horse?" "Well, come and see." I took him into
the playroom where the horse was and showed him the
beautiful tail. "Do you know where I got the tail?"
I said. "That's part of Barney's tail." "It is not!"
said Johnny. "All right, come out and I'll show you",
said I.   Out we both went to where Barney was standing
in the yard, lifted up his tail and sure enough, there
was the evidence where quite a large tuft of hair had
been removed. The remark that Johnny made at that time
does not bear repeating. However, he took the joke and
Barney's tail transferred to our wooden horse is still
a conversation piece.

*   *   *   *   *

The Woman's Association in the church one year
decided that they would produce a play. The one they
chose was called "Packing the Missionary Barrel".
It depicted a number of women gathered together col-
lecting articles to put in the missionary barrel to
send away. At one point in the play, a spool of thread
was supposed to be dropped and to roll across the floor.
Somebody was to think it was a mouse, and give the alarm
crying, "A Mouse!" Faster than it takes to tell, all
the women jumped on chairs in a terrible fright before
they discovered that it was not a mouse at all, just a
spool of thread. Bill heard about this play and thought
what fun it would be to have a real mouse. There were
mice in the hospital basement, so he took into his confidence one of the staff, the dietitian. "Do you think
that you could catch a couple of live mice for me? She
said, "I'll try." True to her word she did catch two
little mice and gave them to Bill. He got a large oint-
ment tin into which the mice just fit curled up. It
was rather difficult getting the lid on the tin but
Bill managed it and fastened the lid down with adhesive
tape. The dietitian, Bill's accomplice, was one of the
actresses in the play and her instructions were, when

the part of the play came up where the spool was supposed to roll across the floor, quickly pull the adhesive off the tin, pull off the lid and let the mice go. The reason for having two mice was just in case there should be a mishap with one. Well, this girl had the tin in her pocket and at the crucial time, she let the mice go. Imagine the consternation and alarm when the women saw that it was a real mouse! One escaped into the audience which created a good deal of scuffling, and alarming squeals down there. The other ran around the stage, whereupon the women jumped on their chairs as they had been practising to do but this time they were not acting! Their fright was real! It took some time before the cast and the audience settled down. One woman telling about it later said, "I couldn't find a chair! Every one had somebody on it - I was desperate!" Bill remarked quietly, "That rather upset the play." One woman who prided herself on being a very good actress forgot all her lines, a terrible humiliation to her. Never before had she forgotten her lines in a play. Somehow the identity of the culprit slipped out and Bill was not forgiven by those women for quite some time.

* * * * *

We had skating parties too, on an outdoor rink. Once a year we had a carnival with fancy dress. One of our nurses had never skated but was determined to learn. She had been on the ice a very few times and was still very wobbly and uncertain. She was determined she was going to go to the carnival in a costume. What would she wear as a very imperfect skater who could scarcely stand up by herself? She appeared that night as a drunken bum with a very red nose and bottle in her hip pocket. Because she was such an unsteady skater, she stayed close to the boards around the rink, taking a few strokes, hanging on to the boards all the way and falling many times. The audience thought what a superb actress she was, taking this to be a clown act. The judges awarded her first prize for the best comedy skater.

* * * * *

We often had sleigh rides in the winter. Bill loved

91.

to take people with him in the cutter with the horse.
Sometimes the roads were treacherous with a very narrow
pathway, just wide enough for the horse and cutter, and
if the horse made a misstep the side of the cutter would
go up on one side where the bank was high so that it
took very little to turn it over. Some of the nurses
have mentioned through the years about going driving
with Bill and never knowing whether they would arrive
at their destination and home again without getting upset in the snow. This was no calamity as the horse was
trained to stand still while the passengers turned up
the cutter, retrieved the buffalo robe and anything else
that had spilled out, shook the snow off themselves and
the robe, emptied the snow out of their overshoes and
got settled again in the cutter. There was really
nothing to it. It was uncomfortable, but not dangerous.
On one occasion when Bill's mother was staying with us,
Bill invited Gretta to go for a sleigh ride with his
mother and himself. Gretta said to herself, "Well, if
Bill is taking his mother, surely we'll get to where
we're going and home again without getting upset." This
was not to be. They drove on a road where the banks were
steep, the horse took a misstep and there was an upset
even with such V.I.P.'s as his mother and the hospital
superintendent. His mother took it in good part. It
was not the first time they had been upset from a
cutter. The snow was deep and soft, Bill managed to
hold on to the reins but was hampered in getting up as
his mother, a large, well-built woman, was sitting on
his head! Gretta suspected Bill of manipulating these
upsets on purpose but I can vouch for the fact that they
were always pure accidents!

Winters in the north were very cold and long but
enjoyable if one wore plenty of warm clothes. When it
got to the end of April and into May, knowing it was
spring everywhere else, we would long for spring too.
There were usually the remains of snow drifts in the
bush and along the fences till the end of June. But
the beauty of those winter days with the bright sun
shining was unequalled anywhere. The dry atmosphere
moderated even extremely frosty days. One morning I
was walking to the hospital in early March on a lovely
calm day, no wind at all, a bright sun shining, and I
was so warm I unfastened the buttons of my coat. When

I reached the hospital and glanced at the thermometer
outside the door I was amazed to see it registering
twenty degrees below zero Fahrenheit! The winter nights
were beautiful too. One year the lake froze over solid
before the snow came which was rather rare. We gathered as many as we could of the hospital staff and others
for a skating party, drove the eight miles to the lake,
made a fire on the bank, melted snow for coffee and
while it was getting ready had our skate on the lake.
The ice was as smooth as glass, the moonlight so bright
we scarcely needed a lantern. We could have skated for
miles without turning around - an unforgettable evening.

* * * * *

One day Bill's car hit a porcupine on the road,
injuring it severely so he got out of the car and killed
it. Having heard that porcupine meat was a delicacy, he
put the animal in the trunk, brought it home and presented it to me. "What am I to do with this?" I inquired.
"Roast it for supper," said Bill. "Porcupines are
really special!" "But Dorothy Marquis is coming for
supper!" "All the better. She'll appreciate a delicacy.
Let's not tell her what it is." "All right", I agreed,
somewhat reluctantly, "but how do I get the skin off?"
"Oh, I'll skin it and clean it", said Bill. "You make
some dressing to stuff it with." So I prepared the
dressing with very little enthusiasm, while Bill skinned
the animal and removed from its abdominal cavity an unbelievable weight of partially digested alfalfa. "The
most unprofitable thing I ever dressed!" said Bill,
"There's hardly anything left." I stuffed the huge
cavity, and put the beast in the oven to roast. Miss
Marquis arrived, and when everybody was sitting at the
table, I carried it in on a platter with all four feet
sticking up. The expression on our guest's face was
a mixture of incredulity and disgust. "What in the
world was that?" "Porcupine!" said one of the children.
"Daddy says it's extra special!" Well, we soon discovered that porcupine is not a delicacy, not that one,
at any rate. The meat was dark gray and as tough as
leather. One bite was sufficient. The platter was removed and a makeshift substitute was served for dinner.

* * * * *

The hospital staff worked hard with long hours but we took a lot of time off for fun and play. We had a great many house parties at our home and at the hospital residence, involving the staff and people in the community. A sing-song of Christmas carols was an annual tradition. Other parties consisted of old fashioned parlour games with a great deal of fun and laughter. These gatherings meant a great deal to all the participants for we got to know one another very well and years after members of the staff have spoken of the fun, the good times that all of us had together. Television may be informative, educational and entertaining but there is nothing that can substitute for entertainment and fun that one makes for oneself.

*　*　*　*　*

We had Christmas concerts at the school and at the church. They were mostly the same children at both and so we alternated. One year the school would prepare the concert and the following year the Sunday School would do it.

There was a family who lived four miles in the country whose mother had come to Canada as a bride, not knowing the conditions to which she was coming. She was very young, just about nineteen, had come from one of the countries in the mid-European area, her marriage having been arranged by an uncle through letters. George, her fiance, had been in Canada for several years. He had taken out a homestead of one hundred and fifty acres in northern Ontario. When this young girl heard that he had all this land she thought it was an estate and pictured herself coming to a large home. George had

Typical
Settler's
Cabin

neglected to say that most of the one hundred and fifty acres was bush and that there was only a small clearing with a log cabin. When the girl came out to be married, to meet her George for the first time, it was a rude shock to find such primitive conditions. She was a very pretty girl with black hair, beautiful large brown eyes and a lovely rosy complexion. After the initial shock she settled down and courageously made the best of it. The husband was not a church going person, but she was determined that her children would come to church and Sunday School so walked into town with them faithfully most Sundays. When it came time for the Christmas concert Elia and Annie participated but it was difficult because of the distance they lived from town, the weather often being severely cold in November and December when practices were going on. One year Elia, the eldest in the family, had the leading part in our Christmas play. I was afraid to let him go home as it came nearer to the time of the concert in case there would be a storm or very cold weather preventing him from getting back to practice. Therefore we kept him and his sister Annie with us for a week or two so that they would be on hand for the practices and for the concert itself. The night of the concert, all the family came to our home in time for supper, rather un-expected, but somehow we managed to give them enough to eat.

Years later when Bill died in 1978 one of the most touching letters that came to me was from a young man in Elliot Lake. It was Elia. He had heard of Bill's death through a brother who lives in Newmarket. He said to me, "I remember walking into town to the office late one night when my father was working in the bush. (He would be eight or nine years old). I came because my baby sister was sick and I remember Dr. Bill hitching up the horse and driving me home, then coming back into town with the baby to be admitted to hospital. The baby had pneumonia and she got better. I remember, too, going to Church and Sunday School and I especially remember the Christmas concerts and how my sister and I stayed at your place for two weeks one year so that we could go to the practices. My experiences at the church at Hearst have stood me in good stead because my wife and I and our family are very active in the United Church

here. I sing in the choir and enjoy the fellowship
of that church a great deal. I feel that it was because
of the start I had in the church in Hearst that I am
as active now in the church here where we live." The
young man visited me later and gave me news of the
members of their large family, all of whom hold good
positions, some with college degrees.

HOSPITAL CHILDREN

15.

Excerpts from Miss Mustard's annual report to the W.M.S.
Board in Toronto - 1938 -

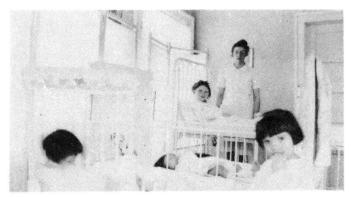

"We have two 'little brothers' who do not have the same father or mother. They are not even of the same nationality, one being Finnish and the other French, but they both belong to God's family so we call them 'little brothers'. The French boy's name is Rene. He is six years old and was very, very sick when he came to us, so sick he was not able to eat or sleep and for many days we did not know if he would get better. His mother lived several miles from Hearst and each time she came to see him he seemed worse so that she hated to leave him although she knew that the nurses loved him and he got every care.

Then one day he seemed a little better, and the next day and the next until he was really getting well again. How happy everyone was and we knew that his mother's prayers, the doctor's medicine and the nurses' care had all joined forces to persuade Rene to get better. In two more weeks he was running around the ward playing with his chum, the Finnish boy. Every morning when we came on duty we were met by this happy little boy who always held his bright little face up and said in his broken English, "Give me a kiss." He chattered away in French whether anyone could understand him or not.

The Finnish boy's name is Sven. He is only eight and for five years has had diabetes, which means that he cannot have any sugar in his food or any candy. He does not have to stay in hospital all the time but every once in a while he gets very sick and comes back to us. After he has been in bed a few days he begins to look for his own amusement and for the rest of the time he is in the hospital, which may be several weeks, he teases the other children in the wards and does tricks on the nurses and gets into all the mischief that any other happy little boy would.

At the time of writing he and Rene are playing up and down the corridors. It is great fun to slide on the polished floor. When Sven wants a treat the nurses give him a cube of ice, his "candy", and he loves it

The hospital cares for many little brothers and sisters of God's big family, and everyone is happy when one after another they go to their own homes, well again.

*   *   *   *   *

There was poor wee Mary Jean whom nobody wanted. We never saw her parents. Her grandmother brought her in very ill with a kidney condition and said she did not want the child home again. We felt from the look of the child that the grandmother probably wouldn't have a chance to take her home again. She was three years old and as pretty as a picture, - fair hair, blue eyes and a round face with clear white skin. She had a great love for pretty things and was very happy to be dressed in clean clothes every day, a pretty hair ribbon or a string of bright beads; her joy knew no bounds. In spite of all we could do for her she gradually grew worse, and two months after she came in she left our hospital, where she had known her first happiness, to be with One who loves all little children.

*   *   *   *   *

There is a baby boy here now who is a great favourite in the children's ward. Two months ago the doctor drove out to his home to get him. The mother rolled him in blankets and placed him on the seat of the cutter beside the doctor to ride six miles all by himself. He was then two months old. The doctor knew it was a trip against death and it was with dread we opened the bundle on arrival. The wee fellow was alive but that was all. We gave him stimulants, got him into a steam tent and worked over him two hours before we could be sure he would live even for a short time, but Ferni had French fighting blood in him. He fought hard for life for two weeks' time, then he began to get better. In another week he looked more like a baby than a starved bird and began to take more interest in his surroundings. Today he is a great pet and lies by the hour in his cot playing in a normal baby way. We will soon have to send him home to a poor one-roomed shack where there are eight other children under eleven. His mother has only been in once in all that time to see him, but one must not blame her. She has many at home that need her and she knows her baby is having every care here.

* * * * *

Another little Czechoslovakian boy, whose parents were very ignorant, was here some time ago. Johnnie had a tuberculous running sore in his hip. He needed long months of hospital care and much good food to build him up. But his parents couldn't understand that, thought he was too lonesome in the hospital and one day they signed the release papers and took him home against the doctor's orders with his temperature 104 degrees Fahrenheit. Poor Johnnie had been long enough in the hospital to know its comforts and he begged to be brought back. He was here for a month or two and then we sent him to Toronto Sick Children's Hospital for special care. He went quite willingly but later he, too, went to a better Home where he would never suffer again.

* * * * *

There was Venna a little Finnish girl seven years old who had swallowed a bead. Her parents could feel it in her throat and they brought her in to see if the doctors could remove it. We put her under the fluroscope of the X-ray and the bead could be seen quite clearly well down her throat. The doctor went after it

with large forceps and to everyone's delight brought
up the bead. He explained to the father that X-ray
costs a lot of money and he would have to try and pay.
He said he had no money but asked if I would take a pig.
I said I would be glad to have a little pig, provided it
was dead, so he brought me one. I crossed his bill off
the books and we all enjoyed the six week old pig.

* * * * *

There were the two little Weibe children, three and
seven, brought in with diphtheria. They were isolated
in a room by themselves and cried so hard because they
were very lonely and also had no English to make themselves understood. The first night they cried most of
the night and in the morning the nurse found that the
little seven year old had crawled over the high side of
her bed, up over her brother's bed and was sitting beside him like a mother. That was the comfort they both
wanted and we had no more trouble with them. We just
left them in one cot.

* * * * *

I think of the little children with fractures
and how patient they are. We have had several with the
large bone of the leg broken and these must lie flat on
their backs for six weeks with the leg in a cast placed
in an upright position, tied to a frame across the top
of the bed. It is just wonderful how content they make
themselves, learning to play and enjoying everything
around them.

* * * * *

Children get some very bad burns, and a bad burn
takes a long, long time to heal. During the last year
we had Guy and Patsy, both between two and three years
old. At first they were very hard to manage and they
cried a great deal. But they soon settled down to
hospital life and began to take an interest in the other
children around them. Guy was French and did not know
any English but soon picked it up; the nurses taught
them little songs and recitations which delighted them.

Patsy was a little Swedish girl who had upset a cup of coffee from the breakfast table over her face and shoulders and she suffered many weeks from it. She was in a burn tent (a tent over her bed with an electric light in it) for a long time. In these tents patients can't see anything around them. Both of these children went home completely healed.

*   *   *   *   *

A young father and mother brought a wee sick baby to us early one morning. The baby had been born in our hospital a month before and we had almost lost the young mother. Now the baby had whooping cough. It took such a severe coughing spell while I undressed it that I was afraid it would pass away before the doctor could examine it. The parents were Roman Catholic and they asked pathetically if I would baptize their infant. We nurses were allowed to do that for them in an emergency, so I baptized it and the parents were so relieved. The parents came every day by dog team, the young mother on the little sled and the father running with the dogs.

We worked very hard over the little thing, but in two days it died.

They had no money for a coffin and when I was preparing the baby for burial, I put it in a box in which flowers had come to the hospital. They started for home, with the mother on the sleigh holding her precious box. I felt that it was a very apt coffin, for it was truly their little flower that was incased there.

* * * * *

We had several cases of pneumonia and bronchitis this year. The children with bronchitis did well under a steam tent with very little other treatment, except good food. Those with pneumonia took a great deal of care, but nursing counted for so much, it was always a satisfaction to pull them through.

We had a lot of children with bowel infections. The favourite home remedy was a dose of salts, which in the presence of infection was the worst thing that could have been done. Often we got kiddies with ruptured appendix, and sometimes, it was impossible to save them even with the most skilled of surgeons. There were also children who were undernourished, because their families didn't have enough food to go around and even when there was, it was indigestible to the children. Many little babies were brought up on canned milk, but it took a good mother to bring up a healthy baby on it without the use of orange juice and cod liver oil, which she couldn't afford to buy. Many a new baby's formula was weak tea with cream in it. When sickness struck, these little undernourished babies had little reserve to fight with so it was a hard struggle to bring them to the stage where they could tolerate ordinary foods.

* * * * *

Wendy and Spricky were two little baby boys, one German and one Bulgarian, who spent most of their first year with us. They were hard babies to get started on life's road and just couldn't keep well in their homes that had so little of the bare necessities of life to give them. We couldn't give them parent's love but we certainly gave them our own and they thrived on it.

They tried home life over and over again but each time they came back to us for another start. By the time they were a year old they were ready to face the hardships of their homes pretty well. During the past year we have seen them often and they are lovely healthy boys.

* * * * *

Francis was a poor little undernourished child of eighteen months when he was brought in. He had never walked or talked, he was pale and listless and we despaired of ever seeing him smile. But we fed him well and gave him some of the comforts that are every child's due and after several months he began to unfold like a beautiful flower. His face gradually took on a happier look. We began then to get him to use his feet for walking and had a pen out in the sunshine for him. As he got stronger he found he could get out of the pen and one day we found him in a mud puddle in the middle of the road. It was not a very safe place to play but it was great to see him a normal child ready to make mud pies.

* * * * *

The children that come in for operative work are perhaps the happiest of all. They get their operation over and in a few days are feeling well but have to stay in bed usually two weeks. They begin to make life interesting around them as soon as they feel well. One young lad of eight or so spent his spare time with a sling shot and some sealer rings shooting them at the nurses as they passed the door. He did not let his bait get away on him either. He had some string tied to each one of them so he could pull it back home. The little girls play with dolls and both boys and girls enjoy the nice scrap books and picture books that are sent to us. They will play for hours with a scribbler and pencil or with paste and scissors making their own scrap books.

Children's work never loses its interests; it always seems so well worth while. We feel we are fitting the children to take their places in life. Their rightful heritage is good health, no matter what other circumstances they have to face. So year after year we look back on the number that have come and gone home healthy and well and we feel glad that we have been able to help them. The children are the future of our race.

* * * * *

I took a dear little girl to Sick Children's Hospital in Toronto last week. She had been with us in Hearst Hospital for three months. She had a very bad infection in her leg. She came to us a poor little undernourished girl of eleven years old, shy and frightened. In a month's time she had grown fond of all the staff and enjoyed the playthings with which we supplied her, especially the hospital doll she never tired of dressing or undressing. The doctor felt she should have a specialist's treatment so we dressed her up for the journey in clothes that came in the bales. There was a lady's very old fur coat which some of the staff took apart and made over for Alice and she was so happy to have it. She showed it to everyone very proudly. We are hoping to hear soon that her leg is healed and she is able to go home. She was with us three months and in all that time her family visited her only once. They lived only forty miles away but they had no money. I sent them word when we were going to Toronto and the whole family were at the station nearest her home to see her and the nice warm clothes she was wearing.

* * * * *

There have been a great many new babies and many of them would not have much more than a 'wrap around' if it were not for the lovely new layettes sent by church women. How happy each mother is to find she may have a whole layette for her new baby! She had expected to make do with the clothes the last one or the last ten or twelve had left and now she may dress her baby up fine. A great many of the women here have a new baby each year and it must be a great blessing to get a layette even once in a while. One of our doctors brought the twenty-second baby to one home during the year and received his first pay, a ten dollar bill. He said they gave him twelve, but he gave two dollars back.

We notice more each year the awful loneliness that the women of the north face. Woman after woman has come in the past year mentally unbalanced, and in tracing the cause it nearly always goes back to loneliness and worry over getting their children educated. Schools are far away, and the parents cannot afford to pay board. Some of these women recover with hospital care and hospital contacts, but others are too far gone. They have faced it alone too long.

The hospital has been over-flowing this past month because there have been fifteen hundred men come into the pulpwood camps and many of them are inexperienced bushmen and cut their feet instead of the trees. But they are learning to use their axes properly and the casualties are getting fewer in number."

The hospital staff went far beyond the call of duty. In most cases the woollen underwear of the lumberjacks had not been washed for many weeks or even months. One of the nurses took it upon herself to launder these 'long johns' and would present them in this nice clean state to their owners at the time of discharge. One patient refused to accept his suit. "My underwear isn't that colour", he said.

BRITISH INTERLUDE

16.

In the year 1936, we began to think about doing post graduate work in England. Bill wished to get more experience in surgery. He had heard of a famous surgeon in London, Professor Grey Turner, who was associated with a post-graduate school in the borough of Hammersmith in London where people from all over the world enrolled in various studies, and this is where we decided to go for our courses. I elected to do some extra work in Obstetrics and Gynaecology and possibly Anaesthesia. In those days one travelled by ship and in October we sailed to England. My parents had retired to England by that time and we were able to make their home our base. They lived in Moreton in the Marsh in Gloucester which was not far from London. Bill and I both enrolled in Hammersmith Post Graduate School for our courses, Bill working under the surgeon Dr. Grey Turner. There was a complication which we had not anticipated. Shortly before leaving Hearst, I discovered I was pregnant. This was certainly not in our original plan and curtailed the length of time that I was able to spend on post-graduate work. However, we were able to spend a few weeks together in London before Christmas. We were fortunate to be able to rent a very nice apartment complete with nanny for the children, Mary, four years, and Margie, twenty-one months. This capable young woman looked after the children while we were at school during the day. After Christmas I stayed in Moreton while Bill continued his classes at Hammersmith, coming home as often as possible on weekends. It was a very happy, pleasant time for me to have so much time with my parents and with the children. We made many friends in Moreton and thoroughly enjoyed what turned out to be a holiday instead of a course of study. Billy was born in the little hospital at Moreton on April the 10th. At that time it was the custom at that hospital and probably other hospitals in England to have the newborn baby in the ward with the mother instead of the nursery as was our custom at home in Canada. This was very pleasant. Billy was in a crib beside my bed and I was able to pick him up and nurse him, change him when he needed it and enjoy him during the day. The nurses were there to help and it was a lovely experience

to have the baby all the time instead of just at feeding
times. Bill completed his course in June after which
we all started out on a trip into the north of England
and Scotland, my father driving the car. When our two
week trip was completed we reluctantly bade my parents
goodbye and embarked on a ship, reaching home towards
the end of the summer. It had been a rewarding, enjoyable few months, but it was good to be home again.

MY FATHER AND MOTHER

17.

When Billy was fifteen months old, word came from
my mother that my father had suddenly become very ill. So
I made hasty preparations to go to them. Chris Bates
moved over to our house bringing her niece Shirley and
was a godsend during the weeks that I was away. She
looked after our three little children, supervised the
housekeeping, at the same time going back and forth to
her brother's house looking after his needs. My father's
illness which came with such tragic suddenness was the
result of an unfortunate accident. He had suffered from
severe sciatica for several days and was due to preach
his farewell sermon Sunday morning, he and my mother
having planned to move from Moreton in the Marsh to
Yorkshire. On Saturday night the doctor injected the
sciatic nerve to relieve the pain and make it possible
for my father to preach the next day. Instead, the
injection went awry, reached the spinal cord and in the
morning my father was a paraplegic, having no use of his
legs with complete loss of bladder and bowel function.

He had been admitted to the little hospital in
Moreton where Billy had been born. The deficient nerve
supply and circulation caused complications, the worst
of which was an enormous ulcer at the base of the spine.
It was obvious that my father's recovery, if indeed he
did recover, was going to be a long, slow process and I
was anxious to take him home to Canada. I was unhappy
with the treatment he was receiving and had a feeling
that his only chance was with the nursing care in our
own hospital. Also on my own behalf I was anxious to
get home to Bill and the children. I got in touch with
Bill who urged me to set sail as soon as I felt it was
feasible. The doctor in Moreton had no desire to keep
this long term patient and encouraged me to make arrangements to move him. His condition, though critical,
was unchanged and I decided there was nothing to be
gained by delaying any longer. During all these weeks
my mother's strong Christian faith upheld her. Certainly she was well aware of the gravity of the situation
but not once did she break down or show any sign of
succumbing to the strain.

I arranged for the shipping of the furniture and

other household effects to Canada and booked passage
for ourselves to Montreal, where Bill promised to meet
us. It must be remembered that this was before the days
of common air travel. The voyage was a nightmare, my
father spending the whole time in the ship's hospital.
Infection from the ulcer spread, absorption from it
almost caused his death. What a relief it was to see
Bill in Montreal and to have someone with whom I could
share my worries! My father remembered practically
nothing of the voyage or the train journey from Montreal
to Hearst. His life hung in the balance for weeks
and it was only devoted and careful nursing by St. Paul's
nurses that pulled him through. Nerve tissue will re-
generate but it is the slowest tissue in the body to do
so. It was a long and painstaking process but my
father was a wonderful patient and was determined to
get well. He was gentle, considerate, thoughtful for
his nurses, grateful for what was done for him, - never
impatient. In the early days of his illness before he
was up and around, a misguided, well meaning person, in
an attempt at occupational therapy got him started at
knitting a scarf. He dutifully did it to please his
nurse but it was all wrong for him. His hands looked
so large and clumsy and he certainly was not enjoying
it. Later a wiser nurse suggested a Bible study class
and every week a group of five or six gathered around
the bed while my father in his 'true' role conducted a
study of passages from the Bible in his own inimitable
way to a very appreciative audience. We had a hospital
bed at home where he convalesced for months after leaving hospital, with a nurse coming every day. Gradually
some sensation began to return to his legs and feet and
at last the day came when he was allowed to attempt a
few steps. After that nothing could hold him back. He
practised walking every day - at first just going around
the bed, adding daily to the number of times until he
had his first walk outside. The bowel and bladder
function partially returned but had to be constantly
watched to prevent infection. As the nerve tissue and
circulation were still far from normal, ulceration in
the feet was a constant worry. The heels were the most
vulnerable and the tissue would break down every few
weeks. If we caught it in time healing would take place

in a reasonably short time.

After about eighteen months we felt that my parents would be able to manage on their own, whereupon Bill had a house built for them across the road from where we lived. They moved into their new little house where they were very happy and it was close enough that we were able to give them the support they needed. All this time Chris had been a source of wonderful help and encouragement. My father was well enough to attend Presbytery meetings now and then which he loved. This would necessitate a train trip of a few hours. He was guilty several times of hiding the fact of trouble in his heel until the meeting was over. He would say to me, "I wish you would look at my heel. I think it is ulcerated again." To my horror there would be a large ulcer. I would say, "This hasn't just come now. How long has it been there?" I never got a direct answer to that. Of course it had been there before the meeting but if he had told me he would have been kept off his feet which would mean he would miss the meeting. Of course it took three times as long to heal. At these times he was not such an ideal patient and we would catch him walking on the infected foot. He had crutches that he was supposed to use to keep weight off the bad foot and many times I would go into the room where he would be sitting on one side of the room with the crutches on the other which told their own tale. Except for this forgivable naughtiness my father was an inspiration to all of us. He had times of depression - no wonder when he had thought nothing of walking five miles at a stretch before he was afflicted thus.

My father's hobbies were gardening and bee keeping. I can remember his bee hives from the time I was a small child. Modern bee keepers know when a queen bee is mature and move her with her followers to a new hive, forestalling the necessity for the bees to swarm. My father's bees swarmed. The new queen and thousands of bees piled up on a branch at the top of a tree or occasionally, with luck, on a fence post. One had to get up to where the bees were, locate the queen, put her into the new hive, and descend to the ground carrying the new hive with the bees not in the best humour buzzing angrily about one's head. The worst was then over as the angry bees joined the queen in the hive. It seemed

my father's bees always swarmed on a Sunday, usually at
church time. (I suppose it also happened on weekdays
but it is the Sundays I remember). My father, due in
the pulpit, desperately scurried about trying to find a
helper to retrieve the bees who knew nothing nor cared
about church services. If they were left swarming too
long they would fly away and the hive would be lost.
When a new queen was needed my father would order one
from Eaton's. She would arrive in a little flat box in
plain sight through the netting that covered the box,
along with the other letters in the mail.

My mother met my father when he was attending
university in Yorkshire and was a boarder in my grandmother's house.

She was a popular girl with lots of friends of
both sexes. More than one man was especially interested
in her. She told one young man who proposed marriage
that she would never be married because her ideal of the
man she would marry was so high that such a man would
never ask her. It was only a few weeks later that she
became engaged to my father. She then felt duty bound
to go to the other young man and explain that she had
met her ideal and, wonder of wonders, he had fallen in
love with her. Mother was a gentle little soul, a
wonderful mother to my brothers Douglas and Sidney,
sister Mary and myself whom my father affectionately
called Peggy (Scottish for Margaret and later Bill
adopted it as his pet name for me). She was an ideal
minister's wife. She looked after my father as long
as he needed her. The day after he died she suffered
a stroke and never walked again. They had been married
forty-nine years and six months.

Quotation from G. Watt Smith's autobiography
- From the Plough to the Pulpit - 1941 -
"So I close the story just when the golden jubilee
of my ordination is celebrated. My wife, who has
been a wonderful helpmate, has just passed her 83rd
year and I my 78th. I am still eager to serve and I
wish I could live to see what is to be done when this
hideous war is over. I hold office as padre of the
local Legion which brings me into contact with the
returning men. I thank God for all I have been able
to do in His service and pray that I may still be used

until it may please Him to call me from it to the place my Lord has prepared."

Exactly four weeks before his death he preached for the last time in the United Church in Kapuskasing. He was not well and sat during his sermon but lacked nothing in eloquence, his eyes bright as usual and there was the same force and vitality that had always characterized his sermons. Sunday, June 30th, 1946, he died. It was fitting that it should be so. All his life the Sabbath had been his most important day. Always he had gone somewhere on the Sabbath. It seemed appropriate that he should go to his Father on that day. My father was one of God's faithful servants.

"OSCAR"

18.

Here follows a description of the pulp camps to
which I have referred earlier, which Bill visited regularly. One was owned by the Newaygo Timber Company,
the other by Northern Paper Mills. These employed
quite a number of men. At first there were only men,
no wives or children. In later years both Newaygo and
Northern Paper built small homes to which the men were
encouraged to bring their wives, the employers realizing
that it was a much better life for their workmen to
have their families with them. A school was started
for the children and this created a much more normal
life. In the early days, when there were only men in
the camp, there was a very large dining hall where the
men gathered at the sound of a cow bell. There was a
strict rule that there was to be no talking during the
meal. If anyone broke this rule the cook in no uncertain
terms would say, "Stop your noise there and get to work!"
They were supposed to come in, eat and get out with no
social intercourse. The cook reigned supreme. If anyone challenged his authority he would regret it. He
had to be a good cook to prepare good meals and the men
fared well.
At one of the camps the foreman was a tall, very
well built Finnish man whose name was Oscar. He treated his workmen well and was a character well known on the
streets of Hearst. He came to town regularly, cashed
his cheque, frequented the beer parlors and was rarely
seen on the street sober. Oscar was always in a jovial
friendly mood; I do not recall ever seeing him out of
sorts. He was especially kind to children. When he
would see them on the street, he would speak to them,
pull out one dollar or two dollars or sometimes a bill
of even larger denomination and insist that the children take it. In vain the mothers forbade their children to take money from Oscar, because he made it practically impossible to refuse. Mary was offered money
on one occasion. She refused it but Oscar, who would
not take no for an answer, slipped the dollar bill into
the pocket of her coat. One night when Bill was out,
Oscar came to the office, which was at that time in our
home, late at night with an aching tooth. He was deter-

Caterpillar tractor
hauling logs out of
the bush

Stock piling logs at
the pulp camp

Typical pulp camp. Men
gathered outside the dining
hall after a meal

Horse drawn load of logs on bush road near camp

Logging truck with a load of logs in the camp

mined that he must get the tooth out. I had previously
extracted a few teeth, but after examining Oscar's
aching tooth and finding it to be a lower molar, difficult
to extract from any patient, let alone a patient with
the dimensions of this man, I was very certain that I
could never extract that tooth. Oscar was not to be
deterred. As usual he was far from sober but very
pleasant and friendly. He insisted that I get out the
forceps and apply them to the tooth. I did so and pulled with all my might but never made an impression on the
tooth. I said to Oscar, "It's no good Oscar. I can't
get your tooth out. You'll have to wait until Dr. Bill
gets home," To which Oscar replied, "You put the pliers
on the tooth and I'll pull." We tried this but neither
one of us was able to budge that tooth and poor Oscar had
to leave with his tooth still in his mouth, carrying an
envelope with some pain killing pills.

For several years my father took the place of a
student minister which brought him into the position of
a pulpwood camp missionary, a very demanding, often
rewarding piece of work. He took great delight in
visiting the pulp camps, visiting the men, talking to
them and holding a service in the evening when the day's
work was finished. He would spend the night and come
back on the train the following day. One night he had
planned a service in Oscar's camp. It was to be in the
dining hall. When it came time for the service there was
only a handful of men. This would never do! Oscar
was very fond of my father and he was not going to have
his men let my father down by not attending the service.
Oscar went from bunkhouse to bunkhouse where the men
were stretched out, some of them in bed for the night,
some of them just resting. In his great booming voice he
called out, "Come on, you lazy bums! Get out there!
There's going to be a Christmas Service. Get out there
and get to the Christmas Service! If you don't get out
there in five minutes !%&#*" In a very short time the
bunkhouses were empty, the men making their way to what
Oscar described as the Christmas Service, his interpret-
ation of Christian. The men filled the hall and my
father had a rousing good sing song and church service
that night.

"The hospital takes its place in the community as
a haven for many besides caring for the sick and
providing a source of income to many of the local people.
It deals month about with the local stores, it burns local
wood in its furnaces, and it hires local help to some extent.
Its staff of capable women and two men take their places
in the community and they serve in many of the community
activities. We reach many people that the church and
schools cannot reach and yet we serve the church in
many tangible ways, - Sunday School, choir, Explorer and
C.G.I.T. group leaders." - G.M. -

Truly St. Paul's Hospital and St. Paul's Church
worked hand in hand. Bill and I were actively associated
with the Sunday School, I was mostly in the Primary
department, while Bill taught teen age boys for several

years, took them camping in
the summer to the cabin on
Lake Pivabiska, besides the
Sunday class all year. Those
boys, grown up long ago,
scattered in various places
in Ontario and across Canada,
have all done well. I have
met some of them through the
years and as they speak of
Bill they tell me of the
splendid influence he had
on their lives, a wonderful
tribute to him.

During the fourteen years we spent at Hearst eight
ministers served in the church. It was a Home Mission
field. The practice by the Church board was to appoint
ordinands to mission fields for a period of at least two
years and so usually it was over the little manse threshold that the new minister carried his young bride. It
was a "breaking in" period for the wives as much as for
their reverend husbands. Mrs. Packham, a very young
bride, was often frustrated and upset, trying to carry
on her role as minister's wife in the manse where there
were no indoor conveniences, no plumbing and no electricity,
Miss Janetta Donaldson, the superintendent of the hospital,

who was very deaf, said to Mrs. Packham one day, "Some-
day when your husband is away for a day at Presbytery and you're busy, just phone up the hospital and
come over for lunch." Mrs. Packham gratefully said she
would be pleased to do just that. One day, soon after
this conversation, Mr. Packham went to Presbytery having
to stay two days because of the infrequency of the trains.
Mrs. Packham was in the middle of the washing. All the
water had to be carried from the well, or snow brought
in and melted. Noon arrived and she was still not finished her wash. Everything was in a mess. She suddenly
thought of Miss Donaldson's invitation and as it was
just about time for dinner at the hospital, she decided
she would telephone and invite herself over for lunch.
Miss Donaldson answered the phone. Mrs. Packham said,
"Mr. Packham is away and I would just love to come over
for lunch." To her horror, Miss Donaldson said, "Thank
you very much. I would just love to come." Mrs. Packham
was so taken aback that she said no more, just hung up
the telephone, wondering what on earth she would do. She
immediately had to clean up the mess as well as she
could and find something for lunch as the superintendent
was arriving within the next few minutes.

Bob Wilson and his wife Mabel arrived in Hearst two
months before we were married and probably because we
were new to the country at the same time, we became very
good friends. Bob was a brilliant preacher, a scholar,
sometimes over our heads with his eloquence, a tireless
worker, and inclined to be impatient with anyone who
didn't like work as well as he did. He planted a caragana
hedge in front of the church that he was very proud of,
which is still thriving fifty years later. Bob was a
talented violinist, and sometimes played at the church
services. I could play the piano and we formed a trio
with a young Bulgarian cellist. We practised every week,
alternately at the manse and our house. Bill and Mabel
would sit on the chesterfield, sometimes listening, more
often talking. One evening Bob stopped in the middle of
a piece and snapped, "Can't you two stop your talking?"
Whereupon my Bill, undaunted, retorted, "You get on with
your playing. If we want to talk, we'll talk! We're not
going to sit here quiet for two hours just listening to
you!"

Ross Muir was a comic. We thought at first that the

funny things he did were done innocently and considered him rather naive; later we realized that he too was laughing at himself. When he was buying a new stove for the manse he took a block of wood to the hardware store to make sure it would fit. One day as he was leaving to go downtown wearing his coat and fur cap he passed through the manse kitchen where some washing was hanging on a creel close to the ceiling. Ross was tall and as he passed under the clothes a lace antimacassar clung to his cap, hanging crazily at the back of his neck like a bride's veil. He thought, as he met his parishioners on the street, in what good humour they were that day. Everyone he met smiled broadly; some were so amused they laughed outright! Ross loved fires. Whenever the fire alarm rang he would pull on his big rubber boots and rush off to the scene, usually one of the first spectators to arrive. Fires were fairly frequent, especially in winter, in that cold country where everyone had a wood stove. At the Muirs' farewell party when they were leaving Hearst Ross was presented with a fine new pair of boots to wear to fires, containing thumb tacks with the sharp ends up. As he rose to make a speech the boys insisted he try on the boots. Ross obeyed, again rose to make his speech and after the first few words solemnly remarked, "I think I could speak better without these fine boots."

My father was an ardent Latin, Greek and Hebrew scholar. When he was well enough to go to church he was a harsh critic of the young ministers' sermons. Gray Rivers, Morley Metcalfe and Howard Beer exercised wonderful Christian patience with this criticism which my father made no effort to suppress. When the minister uttered some statement with which my father disagreed he would say in a loud stage whisper, "No such thing!" to my great embarrassment.

Howard Beer was methodical and very conscientious, worked hard at his sermons, which he delivered meticulously in too much detail. One of his parishioners remarked one Sunday, "I thought Mr. Beer would never get Zaccheus out of that tree!"

George Kilpatrick, D.D., a Scotsman, principal of the theological college in Montreal, applied to the Home Mission Board for a church to serve during his summer holiday. The second World War was raging and Dr. Kilpatrick said he could not spend a summer in idle-

119.

ness while so many young people were fighting for their country. We were between ministers - Howard Beer had left, Jim Carder was not arriving until fall and the Mission Board sent Dr. Kilpatrick to Hearst. My father and he had a wonderful time; they were like a pair of school boys, both Scots, each appreciating the scholarship of the other. There were no rude stage whispers in church that summer!

The minister at Hearst was responsible for several outlying communities where he would hold services in any available building, the school or private home. The summer that Dr. Kilpatrick served the charge he and my father organized the building of a little church in one of the communities. It did not cost much, mostly volunteer labour. The two ministers had a great time together during the building, raising the money, visiting the families etc. and it was a great day when Zion United Church was officially opened and dedicated.

Rev. G. G. D. Kilpatrick, at left, and
Rev. G. Watt Smith, the minister
of the newly built church,
at Stavert, Ont.

Jim and Genevieve Carder arrived in the fall of 1942, an enthusiastic, energetic, fun loving young couple with fine leadership ability and a tremendous understanding of, and love for people. In Jim's own words: "On October 5th or 6th in 1942, my wife and I went to Hearst to our first pastoral charge. Shortly

120.

after arriving we discovered that Dr. Bill had been attending the sessions of General Council at Kingston. He was back and so I had the opportunity to meet Dr. Bill and talk about the sessions of General Council, and since I had spent most of the week travelling I didn't have a sermon ready. I said, 'Dr. Bill, I think it's your turn to preach', and he preached the first sermon for me as I had not one prepared. He gave us an excellent account of what had happened at the General Council sessions." The young ministers in their first charge tried to do everything just right, worked hard on their sermons, - planned the order of service with care, had the hymns fitting the theme of the sermon, prepared the prayers with special needs in mind - to have an inspiring, meaningful service for the people. The sacraments were solemn occasions. The Sunday that Jim Carder baptized Grant, the son of our local O.P.P., was not solemn. In those days nobody used disposable diapers, and rubber pants over cloth diapers often fell short of the function they were intended to perform. After Grant had been baptized in the name of the Father, the Son and the Holy Spirit and the people had bowed their heads in prayer, suddenly there was a sound throughout the congregation like Niagara Falls. No, the baptismal font had not tipped over. The baby's rubber pants had failed to do their job as Grant was held high in his tall father's arms.

Genevieve Carder tells the following story of their early days at Hearst:

Our First Manse Decorating Spree

Two weeks after our September wedding Jim and I arrived in a small northern town with all of our worldly possessions in our old "Chevie." I was so eager to see what our first home was like that I did not wait to be "carried over the threshold" of the tiny frame cottage beside the church. It looked cosy and shabby. As we walked from room to room we speculated about its possibilities - some new, impressive floor coverings, perhaps new wallpaper here, new paint there.

The busy months of fall and winter allowed no time for anything except keeping the house clean and warm - mostly warm! But when the March sunshine streamed in on cracked linoleum and dull walls, the visions of what

MIGHT BE came to the fore again.

Consultation with the manse committee assured us
that they would be happy to pay for the materials in
response to our offer to do the work. With no experience,
but all kinds of confidence, we started to paper the
living-room. Fortunately, we took the advice of a wise
neighbour who suggested that we select a pattern requir-
ing a minimum of "matching". Those were the days before
"pre-pasted paper", so the preparation and application
of the paste was an important operation. Our wallpaper
pattern did require some attention to UP and DOWN - and
we had decided that one of us would line up the top of
the first strip with the ceiling, while the other guided
it down to the baseboard. We did it all with care -
but forgot one small detail. Jim found himself between
the wall and the dripping pasted strip. If we had not
collapsed in mirth, we might have saved that strip!
Anyway, we extricated and saved one still-almost-new
husband - and the rest of the paper went on fairly well,
with just a few tell-tale bubbles and creases to reveal
the inexperience of the paper-hangers.

After a week of hard work there remained only one
room to be done. We could not call it the bathroom,
exactly, because it was just a two-seater, tacked on to
the outside wall of the garage so we would not have to
shovel a daily path to it through the winter. Since Jim
was wanting to get back to his pastoral duties, I assured
him that I could handle "the privy" by myself. I selected a day when Jim planned to be out of town at one of
the lumber camps, and by noon I had the inside walls
papered and the seat resplendent in a double coat of
glistening white enamel. With a lovely feeling of
accomplishment I sat down to enjoy a late lunch.

Then the doorbell rang. When I opened it, a very
beautifully groomed woman introduced herself as the W.M.S.
missionary who came twice a year to visit the Finnish
community a few miles north of town. She said she had
been accustomed to making the manse her headquarters,
and hoped she might continue to do so. I was delighted
and while she took off her hat and deposited her bag
in the bedroom, I added another place to the table.
When I looked around to ask her to join me she had disappeared. Good Heavens! - the fresh paint in the privy!
I had no time to think of all the implications, because

the back door flew open and I was confronted by such out-
raged dignity as only a strong-minded ambassador of the
Lord in the north can muster. From the torrent of words
that poured over me, I caught such withering phrases as
"irresponsible", "flighty", "complete foolishness."
She stayed long enough to allow me to remove the paint
from her navy skirt. Then she picked up her bag and
left. I got the impression that the manse would not be
her headquarters as long as it was occupied by a young
woman of such dubious competence!

We have papered and painted a variety of manses
since then, but that tiny cottage in the far north
taught us more than any other. It holds a very special
place in our hearts."

A new building for which Bill was largely responsible was a new manse. Jim Carder was the minister at
the time, and describes its beginning in his remarks at
Bill's funeral years later. "In reminiscing I guess I
couldn't fail to tell you that he was the one who initiated the building of a new manse. It was badly needed,
had been for many years. When the temperature went down
to forty degrees below zero Fahrenheit, remembering that
it was a house without any insulation, my wife and I had
to thaw bread for breakfast many a morning. After two
years of that Dr. Bill said, "Enough of this! Let's
you and I get together and have a new manse built."
And so on his way home from the hospital at night he
would drop in at the manse and I dare say we drank gal-
lons of tea as we planned that manse. It was finally
built. Dr. Bill was always one who could give you a
challenge. He said to me one night as we were contemp-
lating how we would raise the money for that manse, 'I'll
give $1,000.00, you (Jim) raise $1,000.00, ask the
congregation to raise $1,000.00, we'll hit the Presbytery
for $1,000.00 loan and $1,000.00 grant and for $5,000.00
we will build a house that is fit for a minister.' And
that's just what we did. The congregation responded,
and a beautiful new home was built. It even had water
in it; before that we carried all our water. Indoor
facilities, and hot water heating! I thought that was
next door to heaven."

About thirty miles west of Hearst was an Indian
reserve, Pagwa River, accessible only by train, a
freight with one passenger car that ran twice a week.

123.

We met the Anglican missionaries, Neville and Alice
Clarke, soon after they arrived on the reserve and in
a very short time we became fast friends. These two
were true pioneers. Right after their honeymoon Neville
brought his young bride to Pagwa, the only white woman
there. She had always lived in Winnipeg, the daughter
of quite well-to-do parents, and the way she fitted
into this isolated life, such a contrast to anything
she had previously experienced, shows the character of
this remarkable woman. She was happy, enthusiastic,
bubbling over with the very joy of living, never showing
a bit of martyrdom or self righteousness, loving every
part of her new life in the bush. If she had not been
so very much in love with her new husband it might have
been more difficult for Alice. Like others who had to
depend only on the railway, the Clarkes came to Hearst
for banking, shopping and medical care and would stay
with us between trains. Alice often came alone as
Neville could not spare so many days away from his
work. Bill or I delivered their children at St. Paul's
Hospital. The first two were boys and Alice would
bring them with her on her business trips, staying at
our house the few days between trains. They were
healthy, normally lively little fellows, enjoying their
little holidays. They were a few years younger than
our two girls, just old enough and young enough to be
a nuisance. On one trip one of the boys threw our
kitten down the basement steps; another time one of them
dropped on the playroom floor a jack-o-lantern which
Mary had painstakingly carved. Worse still, to add
insult to injury, he broke the pumpkin into little pieces
and threw them in the fish bowl. I loved Alice's period-
ic visits - we had so much in common. Mary and Margie
did not share my pleasure! When Alice was expecting her
third child I invited her to come and stay a few days
ahead of the expected date, on account of the infrequent
train service. When I told Mary that Alice was coming
she said, "How long will they stay?" "Perhaps a week,"
I replied. "A week!" cried Mary, horrified. "They can't
come and stay here for a week!" As it turned out, Alice
stayed three weeks while she was waiting but did not
bring the little boys, much to Mary's relief. Years later
Mary and the eldest boy, John, met for the first time
after their childhood days. Mary was a university grad-

uate, a teacher. John was about to be ordained as an
Anglican priest. The incidents of the kitten and the jack-o-
lantern again immediately flashed to Mary's mind. I
believe it was only then that John was forgiven! Neville
and Alice carried on a wonderful mission among the
Indian people, whom they served all their years until
retirement. They knew the Indian language, understood
the people and were very much loved. Neville became
Bishop of James Bay which gave him responsibility for
a very large area. As his retirement was approaching
he planned when this time came to establish a drop-in
centre for Indian people in Toronto, where newcomers to
the city could be assisted to find places to live, employment, companionship and friends. He gathered a lot of
material together to help in this project but died suddenly of a heart attack shortly before he was due to
retire. Alice had worked closely with her husband all
through the years and was as familiar with his plans
as he was. She was asked to carry on the work in Toronto
in Neville's place. This she did in her own efficient,
gracious manner until her age of retirement.

PERSUASIVE POWERS

20.

In addition to his busy professional life Bill took an active part in the community. A new public school was badly needed as there was gross over-crowding in the existing one and the town was steadily growing. Bill was chairman of the school board and initiated the struggle of the building of a new school. It was indeed a struggle as there was strong opposition. "Too costly," they said. Bill had whole hearted co-operation from the school inspector (an old friend from Queen's university days) with whom he had discussed the matter over numerous cups of tea before bringing the proposition to the board. His Queen's friend said, "Go to see the Minister and see how much money you can get." Off Bill went to Toronto where he was very well received by the Minister of Education who assured him of a substantial grant for the project. Bill reported this in jubilation to the Board but still met strong opposition. A public meeting of rate payers had to be called to decide the issue. Bill always enjoyed an argument; he worked hard ahead of time talking to the town's folk, persuading them of the need and urging them to be at the meeting. The opposition worked hard, too. They also had persuasive powers with the added bonus argument of saving the people's money. On the night of the meeting the

 whole town was there. Bill stated his case expressively and clearly, as did the opposition. There was a great deal of discussion on both sides. At last the vote was taken, the ballots collected and counted. It was a tense and anxious moment when the result was announced - Yes! - by a small majority. Bill was overjoyed. He had won his fight. In due time the school became a reality, total cost about $18,000.00. It stands now in that northern

town which has grown and expanded since those early days - increased pulp industry, paved streets, expensive homes, attractive motels and a good highway on which to travel. There are only a few buildings remaining to remind one of the frontier town we knew. This year, 1982, Hearst is celebrating its sixtieth anniversary.

A NIGHT AT ST. PAUL'S

21.

by Norah Taylor - Nurse

       Seven o'clock, and we, the night staff make our
way to the hospital, thankful for the tunnel, which
protects us from the storms outside. One thought is
uppermost in our minds. "What will this night bring
forth?" In a small hospital such as this, where so
many are served in such a large area,it is surprising
the number of different peoples and conditions one
encounters. After the narcotics are counted and the
report and orders read, I make my usual rounds to write
down the census。 This varies little from day to day,
for the bed which was occupied by Mr. X. last night was
empty this morning after his discharge, and now holds
Mr. Y. who came in after tea. Of course there are a
few "old faithfuls" who seem to be as permanent as
the wall-plugs. During visiting hours, the people
come and go and ply us with questions, "Can Pete have
some ice-cream?" "When is my mother coming home?" and
so on in a jumble of French and English.
       When visiting hours are over and the visitors are
slowly pried off their chairs, we settle down to a
round of medicines, treatments, pills and potions, and
it is with a sigh of relief that we turn off the lights
at 10:30 and sit down - maybe to write up a few charts.
       The front door opens, a blast of cold air blows
down the hall, and there, emerging from a snowmobile,
I see a frail little woman and a tall man who carries
a small bundle in a pink blanket。 The father has walked
in eight miles from some isolated cabin in the bush to
get transportation for his wife and child. From the
blanket I hear a weak cry and a rasping breath, and on
opening the shawl I see a tiny little fellow who is
holding on to the last sparks of life with grim determination. The baby is put to bed, and the anxious
parents go out into the night with a prayer on their
lips for the recovery of their son.
       It is supper time! How the time flies! And such
aromas waft their way up the lift! Mrs. S. fills us up
with good things to eat, and strengthens us for the
night ahead. Mrs. S. who hears all, sees all, and tells

nothing, could, I'm sure, write volumes, if she chose to, on the happenings around the hospital.

I mount the stairs to first floor. As Macbeth said of old, "What is this I see before me?" It isn't a dagger either. It is old Mr. B. shuffling off to the post-office, at 12:30 in the morning, if you please, frantically clutching his fast falling pyjama trousers in both hands. Ah me! Such countless steps the night staff do take putting our "wandering boy" back to bed.

Again the front door opens - a woman this time- her face contorted with the agonizing pains of fast-approaching child-birth - call the doctor - to the case room - will he get here in time? - he is here - a few whiffs of chloroform - and Hearst's population has grown by one. It's a boy! And the mother wails pitifully because, after eight boys this should have been a girl. What does one do now? Shall I be sympathetic and offer my condolences, or will I be hard and cruel and tell her to take it and like it? Before I have time to decide the phone rings, and somebody wants to know if this is the Waverly Hotel.

It is 2:30. I waken Miss M., and after a verbal report of the wards thus far, I prepare to take a nap. Hark! What is that? From the depths of the Men's Ward Two comes a scream and shriek that I never thought I would hear in any hospital, at least not at 2:45 in the morning. With two flashlights we rush down to find Mr. B. being hopelessly strangled in the tight clutches of his own pillow - all the while snoring loudly.

It is 5:30 a.m. I arise from the sub-conscious with the aroma of coffee and toast playing ring-around-my nose. For a few minutes the night staff relax and strengthen themselves for the morning run. Another round of medicines, treatments, pills and potions, wash basins, thermometers, and what have you. Mr. C. complains that he didn't sleep all night, although we know he snored loudly most of the time. Mr. B. after wandering around all night, informs you that he is tired and would like to go to sleep if only he could find his bed.

We chuckle to ourselves as we think of the funny happenings of the night. And now we hear, coming up the end stairs the strains of that familiar hymn, "What a Friend we have in Jesus." The day staff nurses are strengthening themselves spiritually for the day ahead of them while on our lips is thanks to God for our ability to carry on through the night which has just passed. The morning report is over. The narcotics are counted again, and we, the night staff, are off to breakfast, perhaps a short sing-song or a run to the post-office for the mail and a breath of fresh air, and eventually to bed for a well-earned sleep.

Excerpts from Reports to Woman's Missionary Society
written by Gretta Mustard R.N. - 1936 to 1941 -

"Sickness is a prevalent thing in the north country
amongst the poor. It is bad enough for the adult, but
for the children it is much worse. The more the child
needs fresh air, as a rule, the more the mother shuts
it out and fills up the stove, until even a healthy
person can hardly keep well in such an unventilated
room. It is all very well for the doctor or nurse to
go in and order up fresh air, as if it were served on
a platter, but it is not very practical. The windows
cannot be thrown up or the room kept at a proper temperature when everyone else in the family has to live,
work and sleep in the same room.

The hospital staff, nurses and doctors, work in
a field that has a twenty-four hour duty, three hundred
and sixty-five days a year, a work which cannot stop
for one minute at any time, surely a work well worth
doing. As each year ends, we look forward to the New
Year as one bringing its own duties and responsibilities
which we stand ready to meet.

A man was brought in suffering from a bite from
one of his sleigh dogs. The bite was a week old and
quite infected. We found that he had a streptococcic
infection, which is very hard to heal. In a very
short time, the whole blood stream was infected and
his life was in danger. The infection spread rapidly
until the whole leg was an open sore discharging pus.
We didn't expect the man to live, his mind had been
affected and he could only move in bed with a great
deal of care. Due to the doctor's skill and the dedicated nursing care, the man slowly fought the infection and began to improve during a period of five
months. Eventually, he was able to walk with the aid
of a crutch, a very grateful man.

Another man broke his leg while working in the
bush. It was a severe double fracture that gave him
a great deal of pain until it was set. The cast was
left on the customary six weeks and then it was removed. It was a perfect knit, but shortly after the

removal, he gave the leg a jerk in his sleep, and it broke again. Everyone felt sorry for him in a cast for another six weeks, but when it was removed it was worthwhile, the leg being as good as new.

The happiness of the Christmas season is still in our minds as we make reports. Our hospital family had a very happy Christmas. The staff devote Christmas Day and much time in the previous weeks to make the day a bright and cheery one for those who have to remain in hospital. A tree is placed in every ward and a large one at the end of the corridor. Very early Christmas morning the staff appear on the wards singing Christmas carols. Then a gift is given to every patient which makes them very happy. By this time the breakfast trays come up all dressed prettily for Christmas Day with the kitchen staff's Christmas greeting on each one. The necessary morning work is then done and it is time for dinner, the crowning glory of Christmas Day. The afternoon is spent in rest and contentment and Christmas is over.

At Christmas time we try to reach as many of the poor families as we can. Many of them would not have gifts for their children if it were not for the things sent to us. We always try to have new clothing and new toys and some candy for the boxes at Christmas. Our Hearst C.G.I.T. group packed a lovely box of Christmas cheer including a Christmas dinner for a poor family in the village. They made or bought the contents themselves, took it over personally and sang carols for the family. Our group is made up of five nationalities and the family they went to are French Canadian, so they are practising "World Friendship". - 1936 -

* * * * *

"As I look back over the year's work and wonder what will be of most interest to our readers I think of a pair of beautiful Czechoslovakian twins that have had to depend a great deal on the hospital for a start in life. They were born here nearly two years ago and have been back to us one at a time and two at a time, many times in two years. We like it best when they come together as one cries so much for the other. They were admitted in July very ill from improper food. We were scarce of beds and put them both in one cot. There

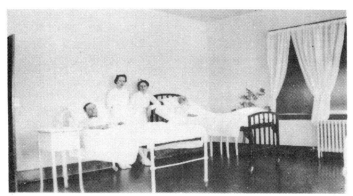

Men's Ward

Fracture Ward: Patient must
lie flat on his back with
leg in cast tied to a frame
across the top of the bed

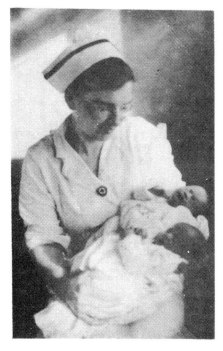

Czechoslovakian twins, Mary
and Annie

they stayed for the two months they were here and as
they grew more healthy they were a great joy to everyone. The parents were very grateful to see them well
and happy again. We wish they might have better care
at home. There is no cow's milk and very little butter
and wee babies do not do well on meat, potatoes and
coffee. One or another has been in hospital off and
on all winter with pneumonia and now Annie is here with
whooping cough and we expect Mary to follow as soon as
she gets it. They are pretty little girls and we love
them. They are very affectionate and soon adjust to
hospital life.

We have had an old lady of seventy in hospital all
the past year. She had broken her hip, and it healed
very slowly, but her general condition does not improve
enough for her to go home and look after herself and her
husband. This is a new country and is very hard on
old people. If this old lady had someone to care for
her she could have gone home months ago. There is no
one but her husband and he must be out of the house
cutting wood etc. and is unable to care adequately for
his wife. So she stays on with us and is paid for by
the Provincial Government. She is very happy and enjoys
the comfort of the hospital." - 1937 -

* * * * *

"Many people live in small shacks and have neither
proper food or clothing for their families. Their
families are large and they are unable to provide for
them. I nursed a woman, who lay ill with pneumonia,
and when she was able, we had many a long talk. I
found out that she and her husband were poor. In trying to give the children the proper food, she had done
without herself, - hadn't had eggs, butter, or milk in
her diet for months. She was undernourished, and had
not seen another woman for months. I realized that with
privation and poor health and constant worry for her
family, how glad she was to find that the Church cared
and would help her and her husband until they got back
on their feet.

It is indeed a privilege to be able to serve these
people who have so little to make their lives happy
and comfortable.

The Indian homes are the poorest. There is an Indian settlement twenty miles east of us and another thirty miles west. Some of the Indian Fox family have been with us most of the year. Katy came first with advanced T.B. She was cared for here for months because she was too ill to move to a sanitorium. Her mother sat with her week after week. She felt the child would die and just couldn't leave her. But Katy grew a little stronger and we were able to move her to Weston Sanitorium but nothing could be done for her and she died a short time later. The next of the family to come was Mary with T.B. Meningitis, a beautiful child who lived only a few days. A few months later the mother came also with active T.B. We were not supposed to keep T.B. in our crowded general hospital but she pleaded so hard to stay that we kept her for several weeks until she became so much worse that we had to transfer her. Mrs. Fox still had three children at home and she felt that by leaving Hearst she was deserting them. It is hardly likely she will ever return to her family. No wonder they feel so hopeless.

There is a great deal of T.B. up here and the Government is working on it. They send in a doctor once a year who holds a T.B. clinic and everyone recommended by the doctors is examined and X-rayed free of charge. The ones found with T.B. are recommended to Sanitorium and sent whenever possible. Most are afraid to go to the Sanitorium because so many have gone too late and have not come back. But if only we can get some of them away in time to get a cure the others will feel more encouraged to go." - 1938 -

* * * * *

"Now of course you want to know of our hospital work in Hearst. May I use this term, "It is booming." Now don't misjudge my statement. I would give a great deal for some remedy to keep people from getting sick, but when they are sick and need care we missionary nurses thrill to the task before us, and the Hearst hospital has been full to the doors - literally - for the past year. I admit that we are working under very adverse circumstances, and it is harder for the working staff than it is for me, but we are together meeting

135.

our difficulties bravely and trying in every way possible
to help those who come to us.

There is a possibility of getting a new wing. The
possibility was much greater before the war began but
we still hope.

It seems to me that our bales at Hearst are better
every year. There is a personal touch to them which
means so much to the missionary on the field. It seems
that the girls and women who sew and work so faithfully for the field supplies must give a lot of earnest
consideration to the work they are doing. They are
truly weaving love with their stitches. Who knows how
far this has gone toward world friendship? One hardly
dares to mention the term right now with a world at
war, but world friendship is needed as never before.
Let us keep right on doing our utmost to bring it about.
That is my special message to the girls and women of
our Church as we start our fall work and study. While
you study, open your minds and hearts to all people of
the world. While you sew, think and talk and pray for
world peace. Think not only of the British people and
the Allies of the British, but think of our enemies at
the present time and let your thinking be Christlike."
- 1939 -

* * * * *

"This fall we are in the throes of a very severe
typhoid epidemic. We have twelve typhoid patients in
hospital with it. It is a dread disease and takes
expert nursing. One of our own staff has had it for
ten weeks, but went home yesterday well and happy."

The typhoid epidemic struck our own family. Billy
was the first; he was gravely ill. We kept him at
home with the help of a St. Paul's nurse. Bless those
nurses! They came at once whenever we needed them,
first the night Mary was born, then Gretta herself
when Margie was born, next to look after my father,
and now to our baby. My mother and father were living with us and Mother, who had been making delicious
meals for people all her life, was inconsolably worried
that Billy wouldn't eat. In the treatment of typhoid
it is imperative that the patient must not eat even
when his appetite is returning, until the bowel is healed

-- clear fluids only - which was terribly difficult for my mother to understand. She had a profound faith in God, as had my father. Although still most of the time in bed with his own physical problems he was mentally alert, and he and Mother ministered to us with their prayers through those harrowing days and nights, filling us with strength with their own strong faith. At last Billy passed the crisis, his fever subsided and he was able to eat again, to my mother's profound relief.

A short time later Margie became ill and our hearts froze with dread as we recognized the symptoms we had come to know so well. Added to the worry was a terrible remorse on my part. I had taken Margie with some other mothers and children to the river for a picnic and the river water was suspect as the source of the epidemic, (although Billy had not been in contact with the river). We treated Margie in hospital which made it easier for everyone, especially my parents. She, too, was very ill. Again strength was given to us from God through parents and friends. The crisis came and safely passed and Margie began to improve. She loved toads and frogs so one day I took a baby toad to the hospital in a jar. It hopped about the bed for a time, exploring its new surroundings, Margie playing happily with it, begging that it be allowed to stay. A nurse who happened to come into the ward obviously and definitely did not like toads! I said I would have to take the toad back to the garden as it would be lonely away from its sisters and its cousins and its aunts, so Margie reluctantly agreed to let me put it back in its jar. The illness left Margie with a heart murmur but as the years passed it apparently caused her no problems and she has been able to lead a normally active life. We have a great deal for which to thank our Heavenly Father. - M.A. -

"The fall always brings us many children with intestinal troubles. We have lost three dear wee tots, but many have recovered that could not have done so in their homes.

The people of our district depend a great deal on what is sent in. Before the bales came this summer we had run completely out of baby layettes. A little woman who has had five babies in the last five years, each one sent home wearing clothes given by the hospital,

came in for her sixth baby in May and we had no clothes
to dress the baby。 We appealed to the Women's Institute
and one or two women got together what they could. After
the mother went home, we got her husband to go to the
store and get her flanellette for diapers. He brought
home three yards。 I guess he thought three yards was
quite a few, or perhaps it was all he could spare from
food for his big family of hungry children. Many women
had no baby clothes except what the baby was wearing on
leaving the hospital.

At this time of the year there are many bush fires
that take homes ruthlessly from the settlers. These
people go to live with neighbours until they can build
again and they come to us for clothing. It is a blessing
to have it for them. They need so many quilts and the
quilt supply sent this year was just splendid." - 1940 -

* * * * *

"One morning a man who had been working on the
Trans-Canada Highway that was being built from Hearst
to Geraldton, was brought into the hospital. He had
been crushed between two machines and died before reaching the hospital.

We knew the man well, and his wife even better for
she had been a patient in the hospital many times, and
the family was one of our United Church families. Dr.
Arkinstall asked me to go to the home with the minister,
since he was new in the area. As we travelled the eight
miles out over bad roads, we chatted about this family
and their hardships. Arriving at the little one roomed
house, we found the mother with one of her children and
six or seven school children that had come in on the way
from school to express their sympathy. She sat trying
to make up some black material into a dress and hat for
the funeral, and as she sewed, she talked to the children. I have never seen anyone as grateful for adult
company as we talked of her loss; she needed to talk.
Following the prayer by the minister, she made us a cup
of coffee in cups with no saucers with the spoons
standing in the cups - this was sincere hospitality.

Two days later, I went to the funeral in the little
church and sat with the widow and the oldest child as

they looked so alone. I went to the cemetry with them
and as they were lowering the coffin I said to the
little eight year old, "You know that it is only your
daddy's body that is being put in the ground and that
his soul has gone to be with Jesus, don't you?" She
said, "Yes, I know. Mother told me."

As I said goodbye to her, I told her to be sure
and call on us if there was anything that we could do
for her, for we had helped to clothe and feed the family
many times before.

A short time later, a box came to me through the
mail and when I opened it, I found a complete outfit
for a woman in mourning. There was everything in that
box, - underwear, stockings, dress, hat and even a new
pair of shoes and new hankies. There was a note telling me to give them to someone I knew who would need
them. Now what was I to think? Only one thing. That
young widow had prayed, and this was the answer. I
never knew who sent the things or what prompted the
sending. I accepted them, as did the young widow as
a direct answer to prayer. Now she could be suitably
dressed and show proper respect for her husband's
memory. The custom in her native country was for a
woman to wear mourning clothes for a year following
the death of a close family member." - 1941 -

PERSONAL GLIMPSES

23.

As the practice increased we required more office space. The waiting and examining rooms in our home were too small for a double practice, and we began to make plans for a new office building. Another reason for moving the office out of the house was Mary. She was now running around and loved to run into the waiting room when she heard the doorbell. To get there she had to go through the dispensary which was very near the kitchen. The waiting patients encouraged her as she loved to talk, and although this was forbidden territory the temptation was too great for Mary. So in 1934 we decided to build an office. Next door to our home was a road allowance which of course had to remain as it was, and we bought the lot adjoining this. Towards the end of 1935 we had a tidy office with ample waiting

and examining rooms and space for a secretary, within clear view of the house. This to me was an important feature as I could see the children playing from the office window. The old dispensary in our house made an ideal playroom. The low built-in cupboards were ideal for toys.

Our house was at the end of the street, next was a vacant lot, then our office, and next door the Bates' house. We knew all the people on the street very well.

There was Mrs. Banks who had a phobia about clothes on the line. We all have phobias - crooked pictures on the wall, too much suds in the dishwater, cluttered counter; mine is toast crumbs in the butter. Mrs. Banks' laundry was orderly, - sheets, then towels and pillow-slips, shirts, pyjamas and miscellaneous things at the end. When she saw a neighbour's washing with the clothes hanging all mixed up it was all she could do to keep from changing them.

Mrs. Holler was a retired nurse, a friendly little English woman with a special talent for visiting. She brought into your home such warmth and friendship that your whole day was brightened. When someone called on her she made that person feel that she was the very one Mrs. Holler wanted to see.

The Larstones had a big family, six boys and a girl. They were active workers in the church, and George a faithful choir member, for years the only male. Kay got all her children dressed and out to Sunday School every week, even taught a class. At our Hallowe'en parties the Larstone children always had original costumes and always won prizes. When it came time for the grand march and judging someone would ask, "Are the Larstones here?" They were usually late - it takes a long time to dress so many. "Let's play some more games. We can't start the judging 'til they arrive!" Kay had a mortal fear of dogs, so much so that she would never go down town alone.

Harvey West owned a large department store where we all shopped. He was Sunday School superintendent for years, and mayor of the town for several tenures. He and his wife Gertrude were pioneers in Hearst, leaders in the community. They had a large family. When the eldest boy heard of the birth of the sixth, his comment was, "We'll have to cut the pie in eight pieces now."

The A.P. Wilsons were great church and community folk. Mrs. A.P. was president of the Women's Institute, A.P. the town clerk. We bought their crib and high chair third hand for $1.00 each, in good condition after their seven children and two in another family had used them.

Auntie Nell Woodward lived across the road. She knit jackets for all the new babies. When she was thanked she would say, "It was just a bit of wool left over." Scores of jackets and booties were made from these bits of wool. It reminds one of the widow's cruse of oil in the Bible (1 Kings 17: 16). Margie and her friend would sit on Auntie Nell's steps, refusing to leave until she came out with peanut butter sandwiches. There was seldom any peanut butter on our shelf because Bill didn't like it.

Mrs. McNee was an outgoing, friendly person. She sang in the choir, and loved to entertain. The Home Mission Board often sent theological students to Hearst for the summer, several of whom carried off brides from our hospital staff. A budding romance flourished between David and Crystal during the summer when the Home Mission Board sent David to Hearst. The following year on his way home he got a stopover at Hearst. He was met at the station, not only by Crystal but a dozen or so other girls who crowded around poor David, seizing and kissing him before he had a chance to even see Crystal who was left on the fringe. At last she exerted her rightful authority, stepped into the mob, grabbed her man, and pulled him away from the teasing girls with a commanding, "Come David!" Mrs. McNee had a dinner party to which we were all invited and she naturally seated them next to each other. During the dessert course the young man slipped a diamond ring on the girl's finger concealed under the table. After the initial shock, Crystal raised her left hand to show us. What excitement! The orderly dinner table became a confused hub-bub with everyone crowding around the happy pair, trying to get close enough to kiss the bride-to-be.

When the American army camp was established near Hearst during the war, all of us entertained the boys as much as possible. Mrs. McNee outdid us - her home was open house at any time to these lonely lads, one of whom came many times and later married her only daughter.

During our years at Hearst it was mainly a town of young people, very few older folk venturing into its rugged life. One remarkable couple were the Reids who had come from Manitoulin Island, pioneers who left their mark on the island and on Hearst with their family of three sons and six daughters. Their young-est child was a pioneer teacher in the north. She was Mary's first teacher in grade one at Hearst, and later our youngest child, Jean's first teacher in kinder-garten in Kapuskasing. Mrs. Reid contracted cancer which later involved the liver, causing accumulation of fluid in the abdomen which had to be drained regularly.

This was a slow procedure as too rapid drainage causes shock to the patient. Bill would go to the Reid house when the fluid had accumulated and sit while the drainage was taking place, one or two hours. As it was a painless procedure, indeed a relieving and comfortable one, they were able to carry on long conversations. Mrs. Reid chatted about her life on Manitoulin where, although not a formally trained nurse, she looked after many sick folk and helped to deliver many babies. Bill treasured these intimate talks, profoundly admiring this grand old lady who along with her husband raised their large family and influenced the lives of so many people. "Well done, thou good and faithful servant." (Mathew 25: 21). There were two people with the reputation of sleeping through the sermons at church. One was Bob Reid, the other was Bill. On the few occasions when my father preached in Hearst he delighted in waking Bill up. He would pound the pulpit or shout some startling word. One Sunday he contrived to introduce into his sermon the word "Glengarry!", Bill's native county. That shout woke him with a jump. He emphatically denied that he ever slept - he could listen better with his eyes shut. The remarkable thing was that Bill could discuss the sermon after church better than the rest of us who had listened with our eyes open.

Tess Sprickerhoff was a person whom everybody loved, - generous, good natured, bravely coping during the depression with her large family. She was a superb actress, threw herself enthusiastically into most of our church plays, in which she found an outlet for a life that was sometimes difficult.

One day I got a frantic phone call from one of the women on our street telling me that Mary and Margie were sitting on the window sill of the third floor window of the house with their legs hanging outside. The girls were annoyed to think that some busybody would tell on them! They weren't doing anything wrong and their view of the town was wonderful.

Bill's love of farming never faded. The first few years we had only one cow which kept the family supplied with milk and butter. In the stable in town we had one cow called Jersey who was quite a pet. She and Mr. Perry, our chore man, were very fond of each other. She had been bred to a black Angus bull and when

her calf was born it was all black like its sire.
Jersey, who had never seen a calf like that, was
thoroughly ashamed of it and would have nothing to do
with it. She not only refused to feed it but pushed
the little thing away with all the force she could
muster. Bill said, "She must think it's a bear." Mr.
Perry said, "I'll talk to Jersey. She'll take her calf
when I show it to her." With that he carried the calf
to Jersey's head intending to placate her gently but
before he had a chance to say a word Mr. Perry and the
calf were both kicked right out of the stall. Mr.
Perry's feelings were hurt more than his anatomy - to
think his pet could do such a thing to him! Jersey
would have killed her baby so it had to be fed by hand.
This was Bill's first introduction to an Aberdeen Angus.

Land in northern Ontario was very cheap at that
time and Bill bought a farm consisting of fourteen
hundred acres with a good house and barn, a few miles
from Hearst. He started out with beef cattle and was
fortunate to be able to find a fine French Canadian
herdsman who with his wife and family moved into the
house. At first there were no purebred cattle on the
farm but later in 1944 he was sent a catalogue of the
Aberdeen Angus breed which greatly interested him, and
in March, 1946, the year after we moved to Kapuskasing,
Bill made a flying trip to Toronto, met Cameron McTaggart,
sales manager in the Angus association, and with his help
purchased his first Angus animals, a bull and twenty-one
females which were shipped to Hearst. This was the
breed Bill wanted. The more he studied them and their
pedigrees the better he liked them and by the time we
moved to Newmarket he had a sizeable herd. The cattle
were pastured in a large field some distance from the
farm house. One year a strange looking bull calf was
born to one of the Angus cows, supposed to have been
bred by an Angus bull. It was brown instead of black,
its hair was coarse, and as it grew bigger its legs
were too long for a pure bred Angus. Also, its head was
a peculiar shape. As the weeks passed it became more
and more evident that the sire must have been a moose.
Unfortunately the calf was shipped to the stock-yard
before it was old enough to grow horns. How interesting
it would have been to see moose horns on an Aberdeen
Angus calf!

Farming was a relaxing hobby for Bill in his busy
life. At Hearst he spent many happy hours helping to
make hay and all year round kept a close supervision on
the farm operations. Sometimes one wondered which was
the hobby, medicine or farming! Patients would come to
the office expecting to see Bill (often with a pre-
arranged appointment). It would be long past the time
he had promised to be back, so the secretary or I would
say, "He's out in the country", not explaining that he
was working in the fields, hoping the patient would
assume he had been called on a medical case. One day
our son Billy, aged five, said to a friend, "Daddy's a
farmer. Sometimes he's a doctor."

The following was written for one of our fun nights
at the church -

Saint Peter stood at the judgement gate,
And with worried look he scratched his pate;
For Death, the rider, with horses fleet,
Had met him that morn on the golden street.
Quoth he, "I am off to a town called Hearst -
Over organization has done his worst
To clear off the surplus down there, I hear.
But he can't finish up without me, never fear,
So prepare you for business -- it won't be long
E'er you will be facing that restless throng.
With grave apprehension, St. Peter took
The ledger marked H from its golden hook
For already up the heavenly hill
There hurried a soul with right good will.
A hive of bees in one hand he carried
And his puffing gave evidence he had not tarried.
"Good evening", he said, as he paused at the gate,
"I'm on time, you see - all the rest will be late."
"Your name?" asked the Saint with questioning look
"'Tis a name you'll find oft in your great black book -
A name that is famous on earth as can be -
It's Smith - ad faciendum, G. Watt Smith, D.D."
"Ah yes," said St. Peter, "we've heard of your zeal,
As a 'basso profundo', you'll add a great deal
To our heavenly chorus. But what of your bees?
In the realm of the blessed we've no room for these!"

Ah, then did the Doctor look very perturbed
And the hum that arose showed the bees were disturbed!
"Of all congregations I've ever addressed
These have shown most response," said the suppliant
                                        distressed.
"So I think of this heavenly bliss they're deserving
Much more than some people that I have been serving."
"Ahem!" said the Saint, "I have just one suggestion -
That purgatory exists, you must cease to question
We'll send your bees there, to make honey eternally
But if once you doubt, they'll be cast out prematurely."
So the doctor entered that blessed state,
And another came briskly to meet his fate.

"I'm a trifle late," the newcomer said.
"But I'd so much to do e'er from earth I sped -
The board of stewards just had to meet
To decide what to do with the surplus heat
From our new church furnace; and the W.A.
Had to entertain grandly e'er I went away.
And anyway, since I've been living in Hearst
I've found it wastes time to be always the first."
"Ah, yes," said the Gate-Keeper, leafing the pages
Till he found 'Carder' writ in the book of the ages.
"One question to answer e'er this threshold you cross.
Those wood-cutting bees - were they profit or loss?"
"We thought," he said slowly, "they'd fill a great need.
So when truck axles broke, and men got bad colds,
And marriage ties threatened to loosen their holds
Because meal-time arrangements and 'home-rule' laws
Were all cast aside for our worthy cause:
We said, 'Carry on, folks, deem the sacrifice worth it,
There's gold for the Church in that wood - just unearth
                                        it.'
For little we thought, as we laboured in earnest
That Toronto would send us that coal-burning furnace!"
"Yes, yes," said St. Peter, "we all make mistakes
So we'll still let you fish in these heavenly lakes,
But to make your atonement, each day you must split
A portion of wood for yon great flaming pit."
He ushered the penitent in, as he spoke,
And showed him, in passing, that pit contained coke!

Then the Gate-Keeper turned with a business-like air
To find two more suppliants standing there.
"Now can you supply me," he asked, "with credentials?"
"I fear not," answered Harvey, "for they're not
                                              essentials,
And rationing these days, you know, is most strict
Wartime Prices and Trade Board has all of us licked."
For a moment St. Peter was puzzled quite badly
This shortage affected his business most sadly
But he scarcely had time to regain his lost breath,
When there dashed up a salesman not daunted by death.
In his right hand a box of gay colours he bore.
"Will these do instead? We have quite a few more;
'Tis true that credentials we sadly do lack-
These are good deeds - we've an extra case out the back!"
At that point Mr. West heaved a sigh of relief
"With George in the firm we shall ne'er come to grief."
By the salesmanship clever, St. Peter was won -
"Those good deeds are of value, I'll count every one."
So the heavenly trumpets gave forth a blast glorious
For "West and Co." to enter, victorious!

As the gate closed behind them, St. Peter did stare
For the next soul appeared stuck on the heavenly stair!
"Ahoy!" called the Saint, "you must come right up here."
"I can't", answered Kay, "for I'm filled with great fear.
Aren't those dogs that I see in the shadows ahead?
If heaven has dogs, then I wish I weren't dead!"
"Come, come," called the Gate-Keeper, "be not alarmed; -
Not a soul on this highway has ever been harmed."
"George left me behind in his haste," said poor Kay,
"And I tried to catch up, - I've been hustling all day!"
"That's all right," said the Saint, as her record he
                                              scanned,
"One so kind and so jolly will never be banned.
So enter, my dear, to this kingdom of ease;
It has nary a pup - you may walk where you please."

For a moment thereafter St. Peter had leisure
Until one came hurrying, not bent on pleasure.
"Good evening," she smiled, as black bag she displayed,
"I have patients in there, I must not be delayed.
As soon as I've settled their pains and alarms,
I must hasten right home - Bill's away at his farms.

And besides, I have meetings three to attend -
Perhaps you a helping hand would lend,
And speak at our W.M.S. next week?
A more <u>interested</u> group you never need seek!"
"Ahem!" said the Saint, quite taken by storm,
"I fear, my dear Doctor, this is <u>not</u> in good form!
Once you enter this gate, you may ne'er leave again
And beyond there lies <u>leisure</u> not known by men.
You may leave your black bag - angels never are ill.
Free time for eternity is yours on this hill!"
O'er the suppliant's face came a look of dismay,
"I'll have <u>nothing</u> to do for the whole of each day.
But I never could live through the ages like that!
Won't you just let me help make the cherubs grow fat?"
St. Peter spoke kindly, with a smile most benign,
"There'll be much you can do in your status divine,
You may produce children's cantatas no end!"
And we've W.M.S. conventions every week-end!"
At that news Dr. Margaret looked happier by far
As for her the Gate-Keeper let down the bar.

When he looked again earthward, St. Peter quite gasped
And his powerful glasses in great haste he grasped.
For ascending the stairway, what in Heaven was that?
He no longer could doubt - 'twas the minister's cat!
"Meow", said the puss, as the Gate-Keeper stared.
"I was left home alone, as if nobody cared;
So I thought I'd just follow my master up here -
I'll act <u>quite</u> prim and proper, have never a fear,
I've a feeling it's time for someone to preach -
I do hope you'll admit me, so the church I may reach.
You see, I've heard so many sermons rehearsed
That in the art of a critic, I'm really well versed."
Before St. Peter one word could utter
He heard from the stairway a terrible flutter
And as ladies four to the gate stampeded,
Puss slipped by the Gate-Keeper, quite unheeded!

"This is most inconsiderate," began Mrs. A.P.
"We've really no <u>time</u> to come up her, you see."
"Indeed not!" with indignation Mrs. Banks nearly burst.
"Don't you know we've a rummage sale planned for the
                                                    first?"

148.

"And surely you knew", said Mrs. McNee,
"That I had invited four soldiers to tea!"
"And to think of that play we're producing next week!"
Disappointment made Tess scarcely able to speak.
"Now, now, my dear ladies, do calm yourselves please!
For you're buzzing around just like Dr. Smith's bees.
This rushing and haste must immediately cease
Or we'll find Hearst disrupting our Heavenly peace.
For penance, on hard golden chairs you must sit
Until in this kingdom of rest you can fit.
Then in heavenly teas and meetings and plays
You each may indulge for the rest of your days."
So the four entered humbly the pearl studded gate,
And St. Peter noted 'twas growing quite late.
But just as he closed up his book to depart,
A sound reached his ears that quite made him start.
'Twas "Come ye disconsolate" sung in grave measure
As a choir ascended the stairway with leisure,
Most wearily Peter re-opened his book
And greeted the leader with questioning look.
"My name is Mrs. George Fulton," quoth she,
"And these, our United Church choir, you see.
We've heard that our only male singer is <u>here</u>
So the rest of us just had to follow, 'twas clear.
Would you like us to sing our anthem for you,
Or could you arrange to just let us go through?"
Most hastily St. Peter lifted the latch,
And let them all in with the utmost dispatch.

"Now," thought St. Peter, "I'm surely through."
But no! One more soul had just come into view.
So again the Saint sat him down in his chair
And was not quite prepared for what next happened there,
For this soul, without seeing the gate, walked straight
                                    thro' it!
"Come back," he said sternly, "this never will do!
You must wait 'till I see if I <u>should</u> let you thro'
When you climbed, my dear man, yon wide golden stair,
'Twas the famed 'Pearly gates' that you crashed into
                                    there.
Aren't they handsome?" - the good saint's pride was un-
                                    rationed.
"Great Scott!" said the doctor, "I thought they were
                            old-fashioned!

But tell me, have you seen Dr. Margaret to-day?
I need her in the office, for I want to haul hay."
St. Peter took on an enlightened expression -
"Now I know who you are, without further confession!
Your record's a good one - though somewhat confusing.
I must confess there is little that's really abusing.
You're indeed welcome here - so enter you may
But on just one condition - you may never make hay
Of our heavenly meadows - they now are preserved
For Dr. Smith's bees, with all rights reserved."

As Dr. Bill entered heaven, St. Peter closed shop
And said with a sigh, "I'm quite ready to stop!"
So he closed the great book, and hung up the North Star
And set off for his home in a cloud-propelled car.

- Genevieve Carder -

An agitation was begun in local circles for an
extension to care for the patients who still over-
flowed into the corridors, to provide the doctors with
reasonable room to do their work, and to give the
staff better accommodation. The superintendent and
the accountant had to share an office in which their
chairs often collided and if a caller came to consult
one or the other, one had to leave. Again appeal was
made to the Government and the board of the Woman's
Missionary Society. Things were conspiring to make the
situation acute.

In the course of time a lighting improvement had
been made by the introduction of a Delco Plant. It
was a help, even though it often failed to function
and coal oil lamps had to be used.

The new X-ray equipment was proving a great
blessing. It meant many patients could be X-rayed and
treated here who had previously been sent to city hospitals, often at great expense and inconvenience.

The need for hospital expansion was desperate. The
number of patients treated steadily increased each year -

           1935 - 832 patients
           1936 - 986 patients
           1938 - 998 patients
           1939 - 1008 patients

The number of beds did not keep pace with this rapid
increase in the number of patients. The total capacity was twenty-eight beds but frequently there were
as many as fifty patients at one time, the top mark
being fifty-three. The overflow were placed in the
hallways, a deplorable situation, terribly trying to
the staff. The climax came one night when it was
necessary to move fourteen beds in order to put an
emergency patient in the proper place. The following
morning Gretta was very angry that such a situation had
occurred. When Bill came in he was just as angry.
Solicitous as they were for both patients and staff they
agreed that such a thing must never happen again. Repeat
ed appeals had been made to the Woman's Missionary
Society and to the government telling them of the over-
crowding and the urgent need for an addition to be built.

The time had come to think of the north as something other than a "no man's land", but there had been no response. That morning Bill said, "We haven't got anywhere with the W.M.S. Are you game for us to do it ourselves? Let's not ask any more. Let's just tell them!" To which Gretta replied, "I may lose my job but if you're game, so am I."

At once they started the ball rolling. A committee was set up and a campaign for money launched. Private citizens and community organizations responded and the building got under way in a short time. Notification of this rebellious action had to be given to the W.M.S. and this was done when the project had proceeded too far to draw back. It must be remembered that the W.M.S. headquarters was six hundred miles away which explains why it was possible to proceed with plans without their knowledge. As expected, both Bill and Gretta were subjected to the righteous wrath of the Board, but it worried them very little. The building was assured and Gretta did not lose her job. It was only a small addition containing eight beds but it afforded temporary relief and by the time of the opening on December 6th, 1939, the Board had forgiven the rebels. Mrs. H.M. Kipp, Secretary of Medical Missions for the Woman's Missionary Society, who happened to be a patient in the hospital at the time, was present and gave it her blessing.

Probably all of us within a certain age group know exactly what we were doing on that day in September 1939 when we heard that war was declared. There had been rumblings for weeks but we had hoped against hope there would be a peaceful settlement. It was a beautiful September afternoon, the end of our holiday at the lake. I was out in the rowboat revelling in the peaceful beauty, trying to store it up for a year, when I met a friend in another boat, who shouted across the water, "Germany has invaded Poland!" We knew all too well what that meant. It was before the days of transistor radios and we had only occasional newspapers brought by somebody from town, so we had been in blissful ignorance of what was happening. The war affected all of us in some way, changing the lives of many people. Tragedy struck our intimate circle very early. Gretta's brother, Thornton, Principal of Toronto Normal School, and his wife were

returning from Britian on the Athenia, which was sunk
September 3rd, during the first days of the war. Mrs.
Mustard was rescued, but Thornton was drowned. Two of
our church families lost a son, one of them in the
Dieppe raid. An American radar base was established
near Hearst with many army personnel, who changed the
course of life in our town on a happier note. Some
were married men, bringing their wives with them, with
whom we formed friendships that have lasted until the
present. Several local girls married and left our town
after the war to become American citizens. Bill used
to say that "The U.S. conquered Hearst without firing a
shot."

At about the same time a camp for German prisoners
was stationed a few miles from the town. When any of
the men from these two camps required hospitalization,
St. Paul's was the hospital to which they came. The
Germans were employed in the bush of northern Ontario to
fell trees for pulpwood, a foreign occupation to most
of them who did not know how to wield an axe. Consequently many were admitted to the hospital with axe cuts in
their feet. The Germans were mostly young men who sometimes feigned illness in order to be admitted to hospital
where they knew they would receive tender loving care
from kind nurses. Having been in only male company for
months, they were starved for the mere sight of a woman.
One could not help feeling sorry for these boys, so much
like our Canadian lads, lonely for home and family.

TWO BEGINNINGS

With Canada at war it was essential that the northern route of the trans-Canada highway be completed at
once. At this time the road ended ten miles west of
Hearst and there was a stretch of a hundred miles of
virgin forest west of the town through which a road must
be built to join with the highway at Geraldton. The
only means of moving troops, should this become necessary, was by train and it is a well known fact that
railways are vulnerable in warfare. In order to complete
the job as quickly as possible, ten construction companies were contracted, each responsible for ten miles
of highway.

St. Paul's Hospital was the nearest to the construction camps taking care of accidents or illness
amongst the workmen.

A very short time following the opening of the new
eight bed ward it was only too evident that a much
larger addition was needed at once. This time the W.M.S.
Board and the government, realizing the urgency of the
situation were in full cooperation.

The influx of construction workers affected the
hospital and staff in a personal, intimate way. The
bookkeeper of one of the companies working close to
Hearst had a sister living in Clinton, the home town of
Estella Marquis, a nurse on the staff. His duties included transporting injured or sick workmen to hospital.
On one of his trips he encountered Miss Marquis, and
upon learning her name introduced himself as Billie
Crookes, whereupon, with customary Hearst hospitality,
he was invited to come at any time. During one of these
social visits to the hospital he was introduced to
Gretta who was recuperating from recent surgery. She
was feeling reasonably well, and had plenty of time on
her hands, a pleasurable, new experience for this busy
woman. They enjoyed each other's company, and Billie's
visits became more and more frequent, no longer depend-
ent on transporting workmen to hospital. The relationship blossomed into one that was to last the rest of
their lives. Gretta's love for flowers was evident
everywhere, especially in the sunporch where she had
planted early spring flowers for indoor blooming. At

this time they were at their very best. The nurses used
to say as Gretta and Billie visited, "The way to get a
man is to take him to the sunporch."

The hospital staff threw themselves energetically
into the campaign for funds. Amongst other projects a
money-making parade was held on Gala Day. Several of
the participants in the parade were hospital staff.

One Friday evening some of us drove to Kapuskasing
and took up our stand outside the bank to catch the mill
employees on their way out after cashing their cheques.
One girl was especially insistent. Attractive, peppy,
and witty, not one man got past her without putting
money in her box.

Cars decorated
for July 1st
Gala Day parade
campaigning for
funds for the
hospital add-
ition

Doctor and his man. Bill rides in Gala
day parade as the man

Two of the hospital nurses enter the
parade driving an ox cart

FINAL ADDITIONS
26.

The building of the new wing got under way at once.
There is no record of a professional architect having
been employed. Bill and Gretta, having already dem-
onstrated their ability in the building of the eight
bed ward, were given the go-ahead to draw up their own
plans, which they did with utmost efficiency. Both
of them had the unique gift of being able to envisage
in the planning stages what the finished structure
should be. It was a large addition, adding thirty beds
to the existing building, at a total cost of about
$45,000.00. The people of the town pledged themselves
to raise $3,000.00, the remainder to come from the
W.M.S. and the government.

Bill was in his element; he loved planning buildings and seeing them materialize; he revelled in watching
things happen. Throughout the weeks that the construction
was in progress we lost Bill repeatedly. A patient
would be ready on the operating table - no surgeon.
Where was he? Out there on the construction site, of
course! We soon learned not to give the anaesthetic
until Bill was in the room.

In the initial stage the sunporch (the man-trap
referred to previously) was torn down, along with the
men's ward to make room for the new building. In addition, a great deal of the old structure was remodelled.

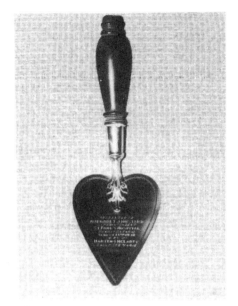

"Presented to
Margaret J. Mustard
Superintendent
St. Paul's Hospital
Hearst, Ontario
August 14th, 1940
by
Harten & McLarty
Sault Ste. Marie

Silver trowel that laid
the cornerstone

Laying of the cornerstone August 14th, 1940.
Front left - Dr. Margaret Arkinstall (seated),
Gretta Mustard R.N., Dr. William Arkinstall
(standing). On right side of picture - Mr.
Harten, Dr. Aubin, E.R. Tucker, Dr. G. Watt
Smith addressing the people of the community
who attended

Margaret and Gretta relax in the new library

Completed hospital addition and renovation to the older parts of the building and the enlargement of nurses residence

St. Paul's Hospital, Woman's Missionary Society

At completion, it was a fine building, containing sixty-
five beds, separate offices for the superintendent
and accountant, a good waiting room, a doctor's lounge
and library, X-ray department, and storage space in the
large basement. The staff residence which had been
built in 1930 was enlarged from a one to a two storey
building.

The corner stone laying of the extension took place
in beautiful weather in August, 1940, attended by four
hundred people. Gretta performed the ceremony with a
silver trowel, presented to her by Mr. Harten, the
representative of the firm of Harten and McLarty of
Sault Ste. Marie. Bill presided and addresses were
given by Messrs. J.A. Habel, M.L.A., E.R. Tucker, the
magistrate, Dr. Aubin and my father, Dr. G. Watt Smith.

The medical staff consisted of Dr. Aubin, who had
been connected with the hospital almost from its begin-
ning, Dr. P. Chalykoff and Drs. William and Margaret
Arkinstall. The hospital superintendent was Margaret
(Gretta) Mustard R.N. The staff of nurses included
Misses E. Marquis, D. Hill, E.M. Wilson, L. Youngblutt,
C. Smirl, M. Twiname, E. Aubin, E. Smirl and M. Dey;
Miss M. Graham was the dietitian, and Miss D. Stranks,
bookkeeper. The helpers were H. Holler, E. Bryant, M.
McNeill, C. Begin, G. Begin, H. Leivo, and B. Reihe.
The three kitchen maids were J. Begin, J. Fulton and
M. Loucks, and A. Ewasiuk was the housekeeper. The

laundry staff included Mrs. Joutsi,
Mrs. Heitala and Mrs. Dwyer. Miss
D. Guest was the student dietitian.
Messrs. Oliver and Jones were the
engine men, Mr. Woodward the
electrician, and Harry Wasyluk the
handy man for the garden and other
duties.

The extension was completed,
duly opened and dedicated June 18th,
1941. The dedication ceremony
marked Gretta's last official con-
nection with the hospital; she was
soon to be the head of her own home,
no more Mustard, but Crookes. Gretta
left Hearst a few days following the
dedication. Her departure ended a
precious epoch in our lives. In
the eight years she had been our

160.

superintendent we shared many experiences, happy and sad, which had brought us very close together. While rejoicing with her in her new found happiness, and realizing that changes are inevitable, we had a great sense of loss. We could not help wishing fate had allowed her to stay long enough to enjoy the new building which she had helped to create.

The following is the address read to her at the farewell party:

St. Paul's Hospital

HEARST, ONTARIO
CANADA

"The staff of St. Paul's Hospital has a few things to say to you. In the last few days you have undoubtedly received many good wishes and a good deal of advice. So we would like to add ours. We feel we are especially qualified to give good advice for we have discussed married women's problems so often and so fully around the dining room table that we have come to some remarkable conclusions and feel we have some ideas that have never been tried on husbands. We regret the worthy husband to be is not with us but he really made good use of the golden moments he spent in Hearst.

Since Miss Mustard is about to vanish mysteriously from the earth where she will never be known again, we decided to take advantage of the time when she is still Miss Mustard to express our appreciation of a beloved superintendent. We hope you don't think we do this because it is the conventional thing to do. We feel rather that there were many times in the past when many of us would have said words of appreciation to you but our tongues clave to the roof of our mouths.

In looking over eight years of service in this hospital you will be able to count many achievements. Everywhere you look there are tangible evidences of your faith and good judgement - the sunporch, the nurses' rooms instead of the old verandah, laundry equipment to meet the growing needs of the hospital, and the X-ray. These all helped to pave the way for the new wing whose corner stone you laid, literally and figuratively.

But we think your finest achievement is what you
have meant to the community and particularly your staff,
those now on the staff and those who have gone to other
work. You have created and maintained the atmosphere of
the hospital. When patients have sometimes told us how
well they were treated or when we heard the praises of
the hospital sung high we have had the honesty to know
just where the praise was due.

We think there has not been one person on the staff
who could not recall some personal kindness you have done
to them. We dare not say we are sorry you are going
from us - but every parting must have its tinge of sadness. Our chief feeling today is rejoicing in your
happiness and we give you heartily all good wishes for
every good thing you can ever wish for and may God
bless you."

* * * * *

Quoted from Gretta's diary:

"Our wedding on Saturday June 28th was in my brother
Charlie's home in Toronto. I had made my own wedding
dress of dusky pink taffetta with overdress of silk net
the same shade. Mary's (Charlie's daughter) was of the
same taffetta, both floor length. My flowers were pale
pink carnations and pink cornflowers and baby's breath.
Mary's were pink and blue delphiniums.

At the first bar of the wedding march (played by
a fifteen year old friend of Mary), Mary started down the
stairs, and I followed at what I presumed was the right
distance. We were both afraid we would trip on our
long dresses, so we couldn't look up at all on the stairs,
but when I got to the foot my brother John was waiting
for me with his beaming smile to give me away.

My brother, the minister, was just grand. I looked
him straight in the eyes all through the ceremony and I
never knew before what lovely eyes he has.

We went upstairs to sign the register and we laughed
at Charlie when he asked me my father's and mother's
names. I felt like saying, "The same as your own."

Downstairs we had the reception at four o'clock.
The dining room table was done in silver and white. In
the centre of the table Mae had a cut glass bowl full of
white delphiniums and five small glass baskets with
flowers

162.

and two pairs of long white tapers and all the pretty
silver and glass dishes for little cakes. The wedding
cake stood on the tea wagon, all dressed up in tulle and
flowers. The knife to cut it was Drs. Arkinstall's
wedding gift tied in a big bow.

We left Sunday morning for Mattawa where we were
to spend at least a week. It is a little town in the
Ottawa Valley, a very pretty spot on the Ottawa River
with enormous pines all around and the Laurentian
Mountains very close, close enough to climb up, which I
refuse to do. We are very, very happy and my husband is
all that I hoped for and then a lot more than I knew a
husband could be."

The following was written by their daughter Elizabeth:
Their first anniversary was spent in Trenton and
the following year they took up permanent residence in
London, Ontario. They at once became intimately connected with Wellington Street United and later Colborne
Street United Churches. It was not long before my
mother became well known as a former missionary nurse.
She willingly responded to an invitation to speak in
her own church and afterwards she was in great demand as
a speaker in several of the churches in London. Her
love for the northland shone through her addresses,
describing her work in Gypsumville and Hearst - her busy
life in the hospital and in the church, Mission Band,
Vacation Bible School, Explorers, C.G.I.T. and W.M.S.
groups. Now that she was established in her own home
her dearest wish was for a baby. Application was made
to the Children's Aid Society with hope and uncertainty
as both my mother and father were older than most parents
who applied for a child. What joy and excitement when
their request was granted! Children had always been
centremost in all my mother's loves and now she and my
dad had been granted the best of all gifts, a chosen
child.
I was their little four month old baby girl and as
I grew I know I enriched their lives. Although my pre-
teen and teen years had their ups and downs we weathered
the storms together and I look back at those days with
a warm feeling of appreciation and gratitude. Although
my mother was older than most of the other children's

mothers, she remained very young at heart. Her capacity
for love, patience and understanding were the exception-
al qualities which carried her through the restless
years of my young adult life. She taught me all the
fine things in life and as I was an only child in my
own home, 'Auntie Margaret' and 'Uncle Bill' showed me
the busy life of a large family with jobs and responsibilities. I learned how to swim, ride a horse, work
in the garden and compete with one's peers.

After my father retired they lived quietly in their
home. How they loved to have old friends and relatives
drop in for a visit - to have their grandchildren Lee
Anne, John and Gail come to visit "Nanna and Puppa",
making them feel young again. Dad died very suddenly in
December, 1971 and Mum passed away June, 1972 - missing
him and loving him to the end. As I look back through
the years I have fond memories of both of them. In those
last few years we gained a bond of friendship and became
closer to each other than we had ever been before,
sustaining me through many troubled times in my life.
Mum's strength has given me strength, her faith and
determination have inspired me, and her constant belief
in the equality of all people lives on in her memory.

"IN GOD'S HANDS"

27.

Our fourth child Jean was born December 2nd, 1941, a few days before the bombing of Pearl Harbour. I was still in hospital when the news came and I shall never forget that time.

When Jean was about five months old, she had an acute obstruction of the bowel, caused from an intussusception which means one loop of the bowel being pushed into another. This was an emergency necessitating prompt surgery. We knew that there was no surgeon closer than Toronto who was as competent as Bill to perform the surgery on an infant. To take her to Toronto was out of the question so Bill operated on the baby himself while I gave her the anaesthetic. Understandably this was a terribly difficult thing to do. I believe that Bill never completely recovered from the trauma which operating on our own baby caused him that day. She came through the operation successfully and seemed to be doing well until a few days later when she became very ill. Another obstruction had developed which necessitated a second operation. How could we possibly endure that agony again? We knew we must and we were somehow given strength to do it.

The music festival was taking place. I was closely involved with it, as chairman of the committee, and we had worked hard for months to put it across. The evening of Jean's second operation was the date of the final concert, the "Festival of Stars", when the winners performed. I was to sing in a duet. The operation was over but our baby was very, very sick and we were doubly anxious as this was the second operation. Could I go and preside at the festival and sing that song? (Where the Bee Sucks - a song from "The Tempest" - words by Shakespeare). It was a glorious May evening with spring bursting forth in all its beauty, as it does in the north, as if in a great hurry to make up for lost time after the long winter. My mother said to me, "Your place is at the concert - you can't let all those people down. There is nothing more you can do for the baby tonight. She is in God's hands." Those words and the serenity of the spring evening somehow gave me the courage I needed. In the morning Jean was doing well and she recovered with no further complications. We felt God's presence very close to us throughout those trying days. I have heard the song I sang that night several times through the years and it always brings a lump to my throat as the whole scene flashes into my mind.

"It was a joy to see their family at the rather
young age that they were at the time (1942) and the
great concern that Dr. Bill and Dr. Margaret had for
their family in spite of their very heavy responsibility
as doctors in that community at the W.M.S. hospital in
Hearst." - Rev. Jim Carder -

Bill loved to play with the children and gave them
all the time possible in the midst of his busy life,
romping with them when they were little, down on his
knees playing horse, skating and sleigh riding in the
winter, picnics and camping in the summer. Often we
would be packed and ready to go for a picnic or to the
cottage at the time Bill told us we were leaving when
a patient would come at the last minute. Many times the
children would be sitting on the front steps of the
house, surprisingly patient - waiting - for Daddy.
There was very little complaint, just resignation.

Years later when the Dean of Medicine was inter-
viewing our son Bill, prior to his entering medical
school, he said to him, "I suppose all your life people
have been saying to you, 'I guess you're going to be a
doctor when you grow up'." To which Bill replied,
"Yes, they have, and I always said no." His childhood
idea of a doctor's life had been many times not being
able to do the things or go the places you wanted to.

Bill was a champion story teller. The stories were
mostly about animals, partly original, partly adaptations
of stories he had read. He could impersonate the sounds
the animals made. When Mary was four he took her to
the zoo in London, England. He was fascinated by the
lions and stood forever, it seemed to Mary, as she wanted to go to the monkey house. Bill carefully watched
the breath inhalation and exhalation which controlled
the vocal cords of the animals allowing them to emit
such blood curdling roars. Through this careful study
he could imitate them to near perfection. Mary didn't
get to see the monkey house as it had closed before they
arrived because her father had taken so much time
learning to roar. She never really forgave him for his
'studies'. When the children were little they loved to
get in bed with us on weekend mornings and it was always,

"Tell us a story, Daddy." Sometimes he would fall asleep in the middle of a sentence, his voice would trail off till silence unsued when he would be vigourously awakened and prompted, and the story would resume.

Bill was the one who looked after the sports equipment and it had to be just right. Skates, skiis and bikes had to be the proper size. When he had Rover's sleigh made, Bill had as much fun as the children, running behind as they rode. Many were the good rides the children had. When the first snowmobile made its appearance Bill had a smaller one made for Billy, an exact replica of the one that took Daddy on calls.

We had skating carnivals and Hallowe'en parties every year. Bill usually designed the costumes - sometimes even made them. He was very clever at this and our family always won prizes.

We have always had pets. Our first one was an orange Persian cat called 'Cupid' so named because she was a wedding present from Bill to me. On our honeymoon, en route to Hearst, we had stopped in Toronto. We had a meal in an attractive tea room and while we were eating a beautiful Persian cat walked into the dining room. We admired and petted her, and when the hostess saw our interest she told us there was a family of kittens. Bill said, "Would you like one?" I said, "Of course!" To the hostess, we asked, "May we see them?" We selected 'Cupid' and arranged for her to be sent to Hearst later. She was never called by her proper name; we began calling her Puss which seemed to suit her, and Puss she was all her life. She was a handsome cat with thick fur and a beautiful tail. She was aware of her beauty and especially proud of her thick tail. She would complete a lengthy toilet, washing herself all over, fluffing up her tail and then take up her favourite position on a chair with her tail hanging down where its luxuriant size could be easily seen. Puss was an arrogant, independent animal, not particularily cuddly. She kept the children in their place, and was a terror to any strange dog that ventured into her territory. We learned from Puss that cats are good swimmers when driven to it. She had an encounter with a skunk one year when we were camping at the lake. We bathed her in the prescribed tomato juice and then dropped her in the lake at the end of the dock for a rinsing. Puss swam for the shore

Taimi, our first home helper,
Mary, Puss and Rover

Rover, our 'sled
dog'

Jean on Tony

169.

like the manner born. She had several litters of
kittens, some with beautiful fur like her own, some quite
ordinary like their mongrel sire. When we moved from
Hearst she went with us to Kapuskasing and then to
Newmarket where she died at age sixteen. She was given
a ceremonial funeral, was buried in the yard in a grave
marked with a wooden tombstone made by Billy. He had
just learned at school to use a wood burning pencil
and used his skill on Puss's tombstone, suitably in-
scribing it with her name, date of birth and death.

Our first dog was Rover, a little black and white
border collie. He was a real character. He was
smaller than most of the Hearst canine population but had
spunk enough to match two or three of them. He was a
perky little animal and as he trotted along with his
tail curled up over his back he exhibited such an arrogant air that he antagonized the dogs he met. Perhaps
he made some rude remark. At any rate he enticed them
to fight. He was so small he would have got the worst
of it, but the fight rarely got started. Rover had a
clever stategy. He would run up the steps of someone's house, press his body hard against the door and
face his antagonists saying to them - "You'd better
watch out! My master lives here and he'll be coming
out any minute!" The other dogs never went up the steps
after him so Rover would stay until the dogs got bored
and dispersed, after which he would trot home unharmed.
He was a faithful little animal, following us on our
walks whenever he was allowed. One late winter night he
went with Bill to the hospital where he waited at the
front door as was his custom. Bill was there several
hours and when he left for home, forgetting Rover, he
left by another door. The poor dog was still sitting
on the front steps of the hospital in the morning when
the day staff came on duty. Rover refused to leave so
Bill had to come from home to prove to the bewildered
little dog that he was not inside the building. We had
a little sleigh made for the children and Rover readily
took to the harness.

A familiar sight during the last year we spent at
Hearst was two Shetland ponies galloping down the street
each one with a small boy on his back urging the ponies
to go still faster. Billy had a friend who had a pony
and one day on a call his Dad saw Tony, who was for sale.
From his knowledge of horses Bill knew this was a

'special' pony. He lost no time in going back to the
place, this time taking our good friend, Doug Mitchell,
with him. Bill easily recognized what a clever, safe
animal Tony was, and bought him on the spot. He was
like an excited school boy, could hardly wait to tell
us when he got home. I often chided poor Bill for
what I considered his extravagant spending, but this
time he was well repaid by the excitement and delight
we all expressed. He was an extraordinary animal, with
a wonderful disposition, clever but stubborn. He rode
literally hundreds of children on his back during the
years that we had him and not one of them was ever
hurt. He obviously belonged to a union which controlled
his working time. If there were two or three children
waiting to take turns to ride him each one got a good
ride but if Tony saw ten or twelve lined up he would
quickly size up the situation, give the first five or
six a ride after which all the rest were dumped off
his back. He had a unique shoulder flip which achieved
this purpose. Tony loved water and would seek out a
puddle whenever possible. No amount of pulling on the
reins would persuade him to avoid that puddle. He would
head straight for it and give his shoulder flip which
deposited his rider in the middle of the water. Does
a horse laugh? I am sure Tony did. The children had
untold pleasure out of Tony as long as they were small
enough to ride him, especially Billy and Jean.
      "When I was young, I spent many summers and part of
one school year with 'Auntie Margaret' and 'Uncle Bill'.
There were times when I was misunderstood or abandoned
by the rest of the clan - left alone and homesick. These
were the times I remember 'Uncle Bill' coming to me,
often ready to tease, but seeing my tear-stained face,
would take me on his knee and hug me making my hurts
disappear as if by magic. He took the time to comfort
a lonely little girl and without words I knew that things
were all right. That hug gave me the security and
warmth that I needed. How I miss those embraces now!
He was an extremely friendly person. He had a firm hand-
shake that made people feel so welcome, and a warm bear-
hug reserved for family and intimate friends. He also
had a very quick temper which I often encountered for
various reasons. He would say what he had to say and
you knew that you had been properly corrected. Then

171.

the issue was dropped, never to be brought up again.
His bark was worse than his bite and one always knew
where one stood with him.

Meal times in the busy Arkinstall household were
enjoyable times of conversation and togetherness in
spite of the frequent telephone interruptions, when the
serving would stop, the telephone answered, and 'Uncle
Bill' would come back and resume carving the meat.
'Uncle Bill' always carved the meat at one end of the
table and 'Auntie Margaret' would serve the vegetables
and pass the plates around the table until everyone
was served. If it was a large gathering, as was so
often the case, 'Uncle Bill' would just start to eat
his meal when someone would be ready for seconds. These
seconds were not allowed until their father had finished
his first and then they could have more. This, to me
an only child, was amusing as my father never had all
that competition when he ate his meal." - E.P. -

Birthdays were occasions for celebrations, always
a cake with candles. Years later the grandchildren
wondered why they could never have a chocolate birthday
cake when grandpa was invited. It was because he had
raided his mother's pantry when he was a teenager and had
eaten almost a whole chocolate cake. It made him sick
and he hated all forms of chocolate ever after. Not
knowing this until after we were married, I often
served cocoa to poor Bill when we were courting.

When the children were little Bill began to collect
wind-up toys. When the Christmas displays appeared in
the stores he would buy some choice ones, family and
friends contributing too. Deciding on a present for
Daddy was no problem - a new wind-up toy. The collection
grew until he had thirty or forty. They came out only
at Christmas. Bill would put on a grey top hat, his
father's from the days when he was a coachman in New
York, and put on a display for the children. He would
wind up the toys to have them all performing at once.
There was every kind imaginable - clowns riding bicycles,
a cat chasing a ball, a performing bear, a crocodile that
opened its mouth to an incredible size, a dog that wagged
its tail with perpetual motion, a pig that fried ham
and eggs and flipped them over, and many more. The
children were not allowed to play with Daddy's toys by
themselves and they lasted for years. When our children

outgrew them the toys rested a while to make their appearance later for the grandchildren.

In spite of their up and down moods, teenagers are a lot of fun. One day Mary and Margie told me of something they were certain was going to happen. All these years later I have forgotten what it was. I do remember that I was quite sure it would not take place and told them, "If that happens, I'll eat my hat!" They were right - it did take place and they held me to my threat. So I had to make an edible hat. I found a bowl that would fit my head, made pastry, and molded it over the bowl and baked it, then decorated it with lettuce leaves, carrot tops and celery. Before I proceeded to eat it the kids insisted I walk around the block wearing it on my head. I chose a quiet time when nobody was around!

ONTARIO ADVENTURE

29.

Two of our nurses were graduates of the Royal
Alexandra in Edmonton, Alberta, and had worked in this
hospital since their graduation. They had become restless and wanted a change, and as they had lived in
western Canada all their lives they thought that Ontario
would be a good place to go - it would give them a
chance to see part of the east. Searching the newspaper, they saw an ad for nurses in Hearst - "A busy
sixty-five bed hospital in a thriving town. Hospital
serving a large surrounding area - four doctors on
staff."

"Just the thing for us", the girls thought.
"Sounds like a busy hospital, small but a change from
the Royal Alex." They applied and signed a year's
contract. They had little detailed knowledge of Ontario
and did not realize that Hearst was a frontier town,
quite different from southern Ontario towns. On their
train journey they met two young commercial travellers
who were on their way to Toronto. They got into conversation and it took very little time for the men to
realize how ignorant of Ontario geography the girls
were and how disillusioned they would be when they
reached Hearst.

"You don't want to go to that God forsaken place.
It's a wild town. You can't walk along the street without stumbling over half a dozen drunks. It's nothing
but a shack town. You want to see Ontario? That's
the last place to go. Stay on the train to Toronto and
we'll show you what Ontario is really like."

The girls began to have real misgivings, enhanced by
the terrain the train was passing through, all rocks,
trees and lakes - no sign of a town, the only dwellings
being section men's little homes by the track and
occasional settlers' shacks. The temptation to continue
on to Toronto was strong, but they had signed a contract.
Their sense of responsibility overruled and reluctantly
they told the men they must go through with it and make
the best of it. Eventually, the time was approaching
when the girls were due to leave the train at Oba where
they had to wait for the Algoma Central to take them the
last few miles to Hearst. It had been a long journey,

two days and two nights, made much more pleasant by
their male companions who helped them off the train at
Oba with repeated wishes of good luck and warnings to
watch out for the wild characters at Hearst. The appearance of Oba did nothing to restore the girls' confidence.
All they saw was a lonely station with an occasional
lumberjack sitting on his packsack awaiting the train,
and the incredible amount of pulpwood piled up near the
track ready for transportation to the mills.

After a wait of an hour or two the Algoma Central
arrived, a mixed freight and passenger train. The girls
boarded the car for the last leg of their journey of
about fifty miles. The train had just started when the
man in the seat opposite the girls, with several days'
growth of beard, a checked shirt open at the neck, both
the shirt and the neck badly in need of washing, and high
boots caked with mud, took from his packsack a loaf of
bread, cut two generous slices and proceeded to make a
sandwich with an onion and a slice of balogna which he
ate with obvious relish. When the conductor collected
his ticket the girls heard the man say, "Hearst". With
every mile and jolt the girls became more apprehensive
as the train carried them through more bush and apparently
uninhabited territory. At last the train-man called
"Hearst!" The girls looked out anxiously. They saw
buildings - houses, a hotel, a wide street and before
they had a chance to see more the train stopped. They
were met by a group of young nurses, very enthusiastic
in their warm welcome, asking about their journey,
telling them how pleased they were that two new nurses
had arrived, looking after their baggage, escorting
them to a waiting car and asking when they had their
last meal. In those first few minutes the girls'
apprehension vanished. These were friends just like
they had left behind.

The girls fitted into the hospital family at once.
The hospital itself exceeded their expectations and in
a very short time they felt at home in it. They entered
whole-heartedly into the fun and social life of the town
and while it was not like the Ontario town they had
expected from the ad in the paper, they enjoyed the
year they spent there.

Dorothy, one of the western girls, could speak
a little German so the German boys were especially

attracted to her. They nicknamed her 'Sister Augustine'. One night, Dorothy had her legs badly frost bitten while out skating and was a patient in the hospital for a few days. The boys missed 'Sister Augustine' and would send messages to her via the other nurses. It was nearing Christmas and one of the boys received a Red Cross parcel from his home in Germany, the only one received. There was great excitement as the others crowded eagerly around his bed to watch him open it. It contained a small Christmas tree with little parcels hanging from the branches. It took more than an hour to unwrap the parcels; some contained a small trinket, others had candy, nuts or biscuits. When he had looked at them all, exclaiming over them and enjoying them, the lad wrapped each one carefully as it had been before, hung them on the tree, called a nurse and said, "Please give this to 'Sister Augustine'." When the gift was brought to Dorothy, in bed in another part of the hospital, she cried. The lad had given her his most treasured possession!

The girls completed their year's contract and before going back home to Alberta they visited southern Ontario to see how that part of the province differed from the north.

Bill's reputation as a surgeon had spread throughout the north country and he was getting more and more
patients from Kapuskasing and surrounding districts.
In 1945 he was asked by Spruce Falls Pulp and Paper
Company at Kapuskasing to take charge of the medical
work for the company. It was a very difficult decision -
Kapuskasing was a 'company town' which meant Spruce Falls
owned most of it, - the mill, the hospital, the hotel,
the club house, and over half of the private houses.
The medical director would be responsible for hiring and
managing a large staff, who would work both in the town
and in the camps in the woods. It would be a very different life for Bill from the one at Hearst. Instead
of being self employed he would be working for a very
large powerful company. He would be in charge of a fine
hospital with plenty of scope for surgery, a challenge
which was difficult to turn down. An important consideration was the fact that Kapuskasing had a good High
School which at that time Hearst had not, and Mary, age
thirteen, was graduating from Public School. After
much thought and prayer we made the decision to accept
the offer and moved to Kapuskasing.

By this time Chris's niece was grown up and practically on her own, her brother was about to remarry so we
asked Chris if she would move with us to Kapuskasing.
We knew that sooner or later my parents would need assistance from someone and we thought that if Chris would
come and stay with us she could continue to be a help
to all of us. She readily consented. My parents had a
house of their own a short distance from where we were
living. Chris lived in our home, travelling back and
forth daily between our home and that of my parents.
Our youngest child Jean was three years old when we
moved to Kapuskasing. Due to an accident in infancy
her physical development was somewhat slowed, delaying
her learning to walk. Chris spent many hours helping
the baby to walk and to achieve other skills as she
grew older. Jean was practically Chris's baby which
made the bond between them very strong.

My father died in 1946, the following day my
mother suffered a severe stroke causing partial hemi-

Jean, Mary, Shirley and
Margie - a tea party
with Auntie

- August, 1945 -

Paper mill in Kapuskasing

plegia. She gradually regained the use of her par-
alyzed arm and hand but was never again able to walk.
Chris filled a very special need as my mother's compan-
ion-nurse. She was an indispensable part of our family.
She was gentle, patient, understanding, unruffled by
childhood naughtiness and teen age moods, always there
when the school bus let the children off at the gate.
As I worked in the office most afternoons I was usually
not home till later. Knowing that Chris was there made
my days much easier.

Arkindale

After three years in Kapuskasing Bill longed to
be his own boss again. There was a sort of caste
system in the town, characteristic of many company
towns. It was an unwritten law that the top brass did
not mix socially with the everyday workmen, nor must
their wives associate at the same functions. We dis-
liked this intensely, paid no attention to it and entertained people in our home regardless of their station;
if they were friends what did it matter? We mingled
non-snobbish high company officials with humble mill
employees, a practice that was frowned upon by the snobs.
Although we enjoyed many things about Kapuskasing, we
were uncomfortable with this social distinction. When
we moved to Kapuskasing Bill did not sell his farm
near Hearst. He left the hired man in charge of the
daily operations and he would travel the sixty miles
to Hearst regularly to over-see the activities. He
wanted to pursue his farming hobby in the same relationship that he had in Hearst but in a less severe climate
than the north. For these reasons he tendered his
resignation to Spruce Falls and began looking for a
place to settle in southern Ontario.

After considerable searching we bought a one
hundred and fifty acre farm near Newmarket where there
was a good hospital and an opening for a surgeon. We
moved our belongings and the Aberdeen Angus cattle and
settled into busy practices for both of us.

Bill spent many happy years raising purebred animals,
showing them at fairs. Coaching and watching Margie,
Billy and Jean train and feed their 4 H club calves,
showing them at small fairs and at the Royal Agricultural
Winter Fair, often winning prizes, was a great joy to
him.

The farm house was large, built by an English gentleman about 1850. There was ample room for the family, and
there were large adjoining rooms on the main floor which
were ideal for Chris and my mother. It was only two and
a half miles from Newmarket where we established our
office, so the whole set-up was perfect.

- ARKINDALE -

Large frame farm house built by an English
gentleman about 1850. Gothic design with
gingerbread trim, L shaped porch supported
by wooden pillars with gingerbread arches.
A pleasing T shaped house, large impressive
front entrance, interior boasting generous
rooms with fireplaces in main rooms, large
centre staircase leading to five bedrooms
upstairs.

The first Christmas after we moved from Kapuskasing
we wondered how we could include in our greetings to our
many friends in the north, literally hundreds, news of
how things were going. A note on every card would take
far too long, and at last we came up with a plan. We
composed a newsletter in verse containing news of the
family and our new home, jotting down ideas as they came
to us for our rhyme scheme. We both worked on it and
had a lot of fun. The idea was extremely popular with
our friends so we have kept it up ever since. We have
sent a poem out every Christmas, missing very few years.
We find that some of our friends have kept them all so
that it is a chronicle of our family since 1948.

 * The "Christmas poem" is now a tradition *

Box 1039,
Newmarket, Ont.,
December 1948.

Greetings to all our friends up north,
All our household now send forth;
We often think and talk of you,
And of the things we used to do.

Since coming here we have been busy,
Doing so much it would drive one dizzy,
With carpenters and electricians by the score,
(Or so it seemed), and plumbers still more.

They have built closets, cupboards and shelves,
With efficiency, if not the speed, of elves,
We now have a mighty furnace complete,
Which for warmth and comfort 'twould be hard to beat.

There are fireplaces in dining and living rooms to light,
Which for popping corn and roasting marshmallows are
                                        just right.
The cattle are healthy and sleek and fat,
It agrees with them here - we are sure of that.

So far Bill has not been tending the sick,
He has been too busy getting this place slick;
But a house for an office in town we have bought;
We are lucky to get it in a convenient spot.

After the New Year Bill will hang out his shingle,
And with the Newmarket doctors will mingle.
Billy and Jean go to a little red school near by,
Mary and Margie by bus to the Newmarket High.

We all send best wishes and want to say,
When you motor south on number eleven highway,
Do come to see us, we do hope you will;
From the highway our house is only a mile.

The Arkinstalls

182.

Grandma Smith and Margie
quietly reading in the
dining room

'Auntie Chris', the
lady who affected all
our lives

My mother left us in 1952 at age ninety, and fourteen years later we suffered another loss when Chris
died suddenly. She was a wonderful friend, close as a
sister. She had lived with us for twenty years. She
had seen all the children grow up, and all but one
married, two with children of their own. Her going left
a big empty place in our household.

As time went on and the population of Hearst and the surrounding area became more and more predominately French Roman Catholic, the United Church considered that the time had come to relinquish the hospital to the Roman Catholic church. An offer was made, the Roman Catholic church accepted, and St. Paul's hospital was sold in 1956.

Early in 1968 plans were begun to hold a reunion of former hospital staff in late summer. Letters were sent out, the idea was enthusiastically received, with the result that nearly fifty people went to Hearst for the gathering. Some had not seen one another for years and a happy reunion it was, with many reminiscences exchanged.

It was a joy to see the efficient service being rendered by the Roman Catholic nurses in the hospital into which we had put so much of our hearts. This was our last opportunity to see the old familiar building. On our next visit in 1972 a fine new hospital had replaced the original one.

The new hospital with its name changed from St. Paul's to Notre Dame was built on a different site about half a mile from the original. The patients were moved from the old building May 1st, 1972, and the official opening took place on August 3rd. Built at a cost of $3,750,000.00 it is one of the most modern hos-

Remembering? Drs. Margaret and Bill inspecting the dispensary of St. Paul's

pitals in the north. It has a capacity of seventy-nine beds and was constructed in such a way that two additional floors could be added if necessary in the future

Hôpital Notre Dame

which would increase the capacity to one hundred and fifty beds. It contains many modern features which makes it unique. It is probably the first northern hospital to have central dispatch and storage and a central pharmaceutical department. There are two major operating suites and one minor one, with fracture and recovery rooms. Every patient room is provided with oxygen and vacuum suction. It has a large built-in laundry with a twelve thousand dollar ironer. It has central dictation, public address and doctors' registration systems.

The new Notre Dame hospital is an institution to be proud of. What a contrast with St. Paul's as we knew it in 1931 with the operating room in the basement, the patient wards on the first floor and no elevator! Though very important, a fine building equipped with the best possible devices for service is only secondary in the concept of a good hospital. Foremost is a loving, caring staff who make each individual patient feel important. This is the heritage which St. Paul's has handed on to Notre Dame.

THE LAST SERMON

33.

        Bill died February 21st, 1978 following a stroke
in March, 1977, which necessitated spending the last
eleven months of his life in hospital. Jim Carder was
at the funeral service and was asked by our minister
after he arrived to say a few words.

    Excerpts from Rev. Jim Carder's reminiscences at the
                              memorial service -

        "When I arrived this afternoon and I was asked if
I would just reminisce for a few moments with you as we
celebrate the life of Dr. Bill, the memories come
flooding back.
        Their home was always open, open to the community,
and I could almost write a book on the events that took
place in which the community was involved.
        Everything that went on in the community seemed to
involve the Arkinstalls, whether it was a skating
carnival, a sleigh ride or a picnic. Often Dr. Bill
was the instigator of a lot of the fun. He enjoyed
life, he had fun living. He served his community faithfully and well.
        We knew Dr. Bill as a professional man, one who was
highly trained for his work and one who served beyond
the call of duty.
        I remember Dr. Bill also as a family man, and a
community builder. He engineered the building of an addition to the hospital, the building of a new school and

manse. They were greatly needed, so he threw himself
into the work and saw it completed.
   We remember Dr. Bill as a churchman, - a dedicated
Christian, a leader in his church, on the Board, and
in the sessions in the courts of the church. Perhaps
even more than that, I remember him as a man who was
dedicated to a Sunday School class of boys. In the
four years of my ministry, before the Arkinstalls moved
to Kapuskasing, Dr. Bill taught his class of boys. In
four years he missed twice and on both occasions phoned
to tell me that he had an emergency operation at the
hospital. Every summer we had a boys' camp at his
cottage. His influence reached out far and wide. He
represented the church in its courts, ably bringing
his dedication and a high sense of the worth of purpose.

* * * * *

"Each one, as a good manager of God's different gifts,
must use for the good of others the special gift he has
received from God." 1 Peter 4: 10